MW01252061

Vendor Bid Analysis
Complete Self-Assessme... ____

The guidance in this Self-Assessment is based on Vendor Bid Analysis best practices and standards in business process architecture, design and quality management. The guidance is also based on the professional judgment of the individual collaborators listed in the Acknowledgments.

Table of Contents

About The Art of Service

The Art of Service, Business Process Architects since 2000, is dedicated to helping stakeholders achieve excellence.

Defining, designing, creating, and implementing a process to solve a stakeholders challenge or meet an objective is the most valuable role… In EVERY group, company, organization and department.

Unless you're talking a one-time, single-use project, there should be a process. Whether that process is managed and implemented by humans, AI, or a combination of the two, it needs to be designed by someone with a complex enough perspective to ask the right questions.

Someone capable of asking the right questions and step back and say, 'What are we really trying to accomplish here? And is there a different way to look at it?'

With The Art of Service's Standard Requirements Self-Assessments, we empower people who can do just that — whether their title is marketer, entrepreneur, manager, salesperson, consultant, Business Process Manager, executive assistant, IT Manager, CIO etc... —they are the people who rule the future. They are people who watch the process as it happens, and ask the right questions to make the process work better.

Contact us when you need any support with this Self-Assessment and any help with templates, blue-prints and examples of standard documents you might need:

http://theartofservice.com
service@theartofservice.com

Included Resources - how to access

Included with your purchase of the book is the Vendor Bid

Analysis Self-Assessment Spreadsheet Dashboard which contains all questions and Self-Assessment areas and auto-generates insights, graphs, and project RACI planning - all with examples to get you started right away.

How? Simply send an email to
access@theartofservice.com
with this books' title in the subject to get the Vendor Bid Analysis Self Assessment Tool right away.

You will receive the following contents with New and Updated specific criteria:

• The latest quick edition of the book in PDF

• The latest complete edition of the book in PDF, which criteria correspond to the criteria in...

• The Self-Assessment Excel Dashboard, and...

• Example pre-filled Self-Assessment Excel Dashboard to get familiar with results generation

• In-depth specific Checklists covering the topic

• Project management checklists and templates to assist with implementation

INCLUDES LIFETIME SELF ASSESSMENT UPDATES

Every self assessment comes with Lifetime Updates and Lifetime Free Updated Books. Lifetime Updates is an industry-first feature which allows you to receive verified self assessment updates, ensuring you always have the most accurate information at your fingertips.

Get it now- you will be glad you did - do it now, before you forget.

Send an email to **access@theartofservice.com** with this books' title in the subject to get the Vendor Bid Analysis Self Assessment Tool right away.

Purpose of this Self-Assessment

This Self-Assessment has been developed to improve understanding of the requirements and elements of Vendor Bid Analysis, based on best practices and standards in business process architecture, design and quality management.

It is designed to allow for a rapid Self-Assessment to determine how closely existing management practices and procedures correspond to the elements of the Self-Assessment.

The criteria of requirements and elements of Vendor Bid Analysis have been rephrased in the format of a Self-Assessment questionnaire, with a seven-criterion scoring system, as explained in this document.

In this format, even with limited background knowledge of Vendor Bid Analysis, a manager can quickly review existing operations to determine how they measure up to the standards. This in turn can serve as the starting point of a 'gap analysis' to identify management tools or system elements that might usefully be implemented in the organization to help improve overall performance.

How to use the Self-Assessment

On the following pages are a series of questions to identify to what extent your Vendor Bid Analysis initiative is complete in comparison to the requirements set in standards.

To facilitate answering the questions, there is a space in front of each question to enter a score on a scale of '1' to '5'.

1 Strongly Disagree

2 Disagree

3 Neutral

4 Agree

5 Strongly Agree

Read the question and rate it with the following in front of mind:

'In my belief, the answer to this question is clearly defined'.

There are two ways in which you can choose to interpret this statement;
1. how aware are you that the answer to the question is clearly defined
2. for more in-depth analysis you can choose to gather evidence and confirm the answer to the question. This obviously will take more time, most Self-Assessment users opt for the first way to interpret the question and dig deeper later on based on the outcome of the overall Self-Assessment.

A score of '1' would mean that the answer is not clear at all, where a '5' would mean the answer is crystal clear and defined. Leave emtpy when the question is not applicable or you don't want to answer it, you can skip it without affecting your score. Write your score in the space provided.

After you have responded to all the appropriate statements in each section, compute your average score for that section, using the formula provided, and round to the nearest tenth. Then transfer to the corresponding spoke in the Vendor Bid Analysis Scorecard on the second next page of the Self-Assessment.

Your completed Vendor Bid Analysis Scorecard will give you a clear presentation of which Vendor Bid Analysis areas need attention.

Vendor Bid Analysis
Scorecard Example

Example of how the finalized Scorecard can look like:

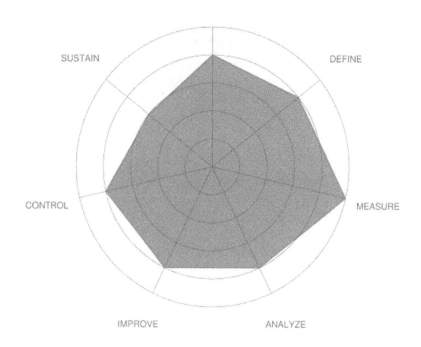

Vendor Bid Analysis Scorecard

Your Scores:

BEGINNING OF THE
SELF-ASSESSMENT:

CRITERION #1: RECOGNIZE

INTENT: Be aware of the need for change. Recognize that there is an unfavorable variation, problem or symptom.

In my belief, the answer to this question is clearly defined:

5 Strongly Agree

4 Agree

3 Neutral

2 Disagree

1 Strongly Disagree

1. How do you recognize an objection?
<--- Score

2. How are the Vendor bid analysis's objectives aligned to the group's overall stakeholder strategy?
<--- Score

3. What needs to be done?
<--- Score

4. Looking at each person individually – does every one have the qualities which are needed to work in this group?
<--- Score

5. What should be considered when identifying available resources, constraints, and deadlines?
<--- Score

6. Will Vendor bid analysis deliverables need to be tested and, if so, by whom?
<--- Score

7. Where is training needed?
<--- Score

8. Will a response program recognize when a crisis occurs and provide some level of response?
<--- Score

9. What information do users need?
<--- Score

10. As a sponsor, customer or management, how important is it to meet goals, objectives?
<--- Score

11. Does your organization need more Vendor bid analysis education?
<--- Score

12. What training and capacity building actions are needed to implement proposed reforms?
<--- Score

13. What prevents you from making the changes you know will make you a more effective Vendor bid analysis leader?

<--- Score

14. What are the expected benefits of Vendor bid analysis to the stakeholder?

<--- Score

15. Is it clear when you think of the day ahead of you what activities and tasks you need to complete?

<--- Score

16. What is the smallest subset of the problem you can usefully solve?

<--- Score

17. Are there any specific expectations or concerns about the Vendor bid analysis team, Vendor bid analysis itself?

<--- Score

18. Which needs are not included or involved?

<--- Score

19. What are the minority interests and what amount of minority interests can be recognized?

<--- Score

20. Who should resolve the Vendor bid analysis issues?

<--- Score

21. Who needs what information?

<--- Score

22. To what extent does each concerned units

management team recognize Vendor bid analysis as an effective investment?

<--- Score

23. What activities does the governance board need to consider?

<--- Score

24. Are employees recognized for desired behaviors?

<--- Score

25. Do you need to avoid or amend any Vendor bid analysis activities?

<--- Score

26. What is the recognized need?

<--- Score

27. Did you miss any major Vendor bid analysis issues?

<--- Score

28. Whom do you really need or want to serve?

<--- Score

29. When a Vendor bid analysis manager recognizes a problem, what options are available?

<--- Score

30. What creative shifts do you need to take?

<--- Score

31. How do you take a forward-looking perspective in identifying Vendor bid analysis research related to market response and models?

<--- Score

32. How are training requirements identified?
<--- Score

33. Are employees recognized or rewarded for performance that demonstrates the highest levels of integrity?
<--- Score

34. How can auditing be a preventative security measure?
<--- Score

35. What Vendor bid analysis events should you attend?
<--- Score

36. How do you recognize an Vendor bid analysis objection?
<--- Score

37. To what extent would your organization benefit from being recognized as a award recipient?
<--- Score

38. What Vendor bid analysis problem should be solved?
<--- Score

39. How do you assess your Vendor bid analysis workforce capability and capacity needs, including skills, competencies, and staffing levels?
<--- Score

40. What situation(s) led to this Vendor bid analysis Self Assessment?
<--- Score

41. What Vendor bid analysis capabilities do you need?
<--- Score

42. What needs to stay?
<--- Score

43. Are losses recognized in a timely manner?
<--- Score

44. What do you need to start doing?
<--- Score

45. Think about the people you identified for your Vendor bid analysis project and the project responsibilities you would assign to them, what kind of training do you think they would need to perform these responsibilities effectively?
<--- Score

46. What are the Vendor bid analysis resources needed?
<--- Score

47. Why is this needed?
<--- Score

48. What resources or support might you need?
<--- Score

49. What would happen if Vendor bid analysis weren't done?
<--- Score

50. How are you going to measure success?

<--- Score

51. Can management personnel recognize the monetary benefit of Vendor bid analysis?
<--- Score

52. What vendors make products that address the Vendor bid analysis needs?
<--- Score

53. Is it needed?
<--- Score

54. Where do you need to exercise leadership?
<--- Score

55. Will it solve real problems?
<--- Score

56. What are the stakeholder objectives to be achieved with Vendor bid analysis?
<--- Score

57. What Vendor bid analysis coordination do you need?
<--- Score

58. Are there any revenue recognition issues?
<--- Score

59. Do you recognize Vendor bid analysis achievements?
<--- Score

60. Who are your key stakeholders who need to sign off?

<--- Score

61. Who else hopes to benefit from it?
<--- Score

62. What is the problem and/or vulnerability?
<--- Score

63. What is the problem or issue?
<--- Score

64. For your Vendor bid analysis project, identify and describe the business environment, is there more than one layer to the business environment?
<--- Score

65. How much are sponsors, customers, partners, stakeholders involved in Vendor bid analysis? In other words, what are the risks, if Vendor bid analysis does not deliver successfully?
<--- Score

66. What are the timeframes required to resolve each of the issues/problems?
<--- Score

67. How does it fit into your organizational needs and tasks?
<--- Score

68. Would you recognize a threat from the inside?
<--- Score

69. Does Vendor bid analysis create potential expectations in other areas that need to be recognized and considered?

<--- Score

70. Why the need?
<--- Score

71. Do you know what you need to know about Vendor bid analysis?
<--- Score

72. Do you have/need 24-hour access to key personnel?
<--- Score

73. What problems are you facing and how do you consider Vendor bid analysis will circumvent those obstacles?
<--- Score

74. Which issues are too important to ignore?
<--- Score

75. Are you dealing with any of the same issues today as yesterday? What can you do about this?
<--- Score

76. What do employees need in the short term?
<--- Score

77. What is the extent or complexity of the Vendor bid analysis problem?
<--- Score

78. Who needs budgets?
<--- Score

79. Are there Vendor bid analysis problems defined?

<--- Score

80. How do you identify subcontractor relationships?
<--- Score

81. Is the quality assurance team identified?
<--- Score

82. Consider your own Vendor bid analysis project, what types of organizational problems do you think might be causing or affecting your problem, based on the work done so far?
<--- Score

83. Does the problem have ethical dimensions?
<--- Score

84. Will new equipment/products be required to facilitate Vendor bid analysis delivery, for example is new software needed?
<--- Score

85. Who defines the rules in relation to any given issue?
<--- Score

86. Who needs to know about Vendor bid analysis?
<--- Score

87. Are problem definition and motivation clearly presented?
<--- Score

88. Are your goals realistic? Do you need to redefine your problem? Perhaps the problem has changed or maybe you have reached your goal and need to set a

new one?
<--- Score

89. What does Vendor bid analysis success mean to the stakeholders?
<--- Score

90. Have you identified your Vendor bid analysis key performance indicators?
<--- Score

91. What are the clients issues and concerns?
<--- Score

92. What is the Vendor bid analysis problem definition? What do you need to resolve?
<--- Score

93. Do you need different information or graphics?
<--- Score

Add up total points for this section:
_____ = Total points for this section

Divided by: _____ (number of statements answered) = _____
Average score for this section

Transfer your score to the Vendor bid analysis Index at the beginning of the Self-Assessment.

CRITERION #2: DEFINE:

INTENT: Formulate the stakeholder problem. Define the problem, needs and objectives.

In my belief, the answer to this question is clearly defined:

5 Strongly Agree

4 Agree

3 Neutral

2 Disagree

1 Strongly Disagree

1. Is the Vendor bid analysis scope complete and appropriately sized?
<--- Score

2. What knowledge or experience is required?
<--- Score

3. What are the core elements of the Vendor bid analysis business case?

<--- Score

4. Have all of the relationships been defined properly?
<--- Score

5. Who defines (or who defined) the rules and roles?
<--- Score

6. How does the Vendor bid analysis manager ensure against scope creep?
<--- Score

7. Has/have the customer(s) been identified?
<--- Score

8. What is the scope of Vendor bid analysis?
<--- Score

9. What is out-of-scope initially?
<--- Score

10. Are all requirements met?
<--- Score

11. Is special Vendor bid analysis user knowledge required?
<--- Score

12. Has anyone else (internal or external to the group) attempted to solve this problem or a similar one before? If so, what knowledge can be leveraged from these previous efforts?
<--- Score

13. Is the team adequately staffed with the desired cross-functionality? If not, what additional resources

are available to the team?
<--- Score

14. What are the Vendor bid analysis use cases?
<--- Score

15. Do you all define Vendor bid analysis in the same way?
<--- Score

16. How do you catch Vendor bid analysis definition inconsistencies?
<--- Score

17. What are the compelling stakeholder reasons for embarking on Vendor bid analysis?
<--- Score

18. What are the Roles and Responsibilities for each team member and its leadership? Where is this documented?
<--- Score

19. What is the definition of Vendor bid analysis excellence?
<--- Score

20. Who approved the Vendor bid analysis scope?
<--- Score

21. How have you defined all Vendor bid analysis requirements first?
<--- Score

22. When is the estimated completion date?
<--- Score

23. Do the problem and goal statements meet the SMART criteria (specific, measurable, attainable, relevant, and time-bound)?
<--- Score

24. Is there regularly 100% attendance at the team meetings? If not, have appointed substitutes attended to preserve cross-functionality and full representation?
<--- Score

25. Is it clearly defined in and to your organization what you do?
<--- Score

26. Are audit criteria, scope, frequency and methods defined?
<--- Score

27. What sources do you use to gather information for a Vendor bid analysis study?
<--- Score

28. What information should you gather?
<--- Score

29. What are the rough order estimates on cost savings/opportunities that Vendor bid analysis brings?
<--- Score

30. When are meeting minutes sent out? Who is on the distribution list?
<--- Score

31. What specifically is the problem? Where does it occur? When does it occur? What is its extent?
<--- Score

32. Are roles and responsibilities formally defined?
<--- Score

33. Do you have organizational privacy requirements?
<--- Score

34. What are the record-keeping requirements of Vendor bid analysis activities?
<--- Score

35. Are the Vendor bid analysis requirements complete?
<--- Score

36. What customer feedback methods were used to solicit their input?
<--- Score

37. How can the value of Vendor bid analysis be defined?
<--- Score

38. What would be the goal or target for a Vendor bid analysis's improvement team?
<--- Score

39. Is data collected and displayed to better understand customer(s) critical needs and requirements.
<--- Score

40. Has a Vendor bid analysis requirement not been

met?
<--- Score

41. Have specific policy objectives been defined?
<--- Score

42. What is in scope?
<--- Score

43. What are the boundaries of the scope? What is in bounds and what is not? What is the start point? What is the stop point?
<--- Score

44. Has a project plan, Gantt chart, or similar been developed/completed?
<--- Score

45. What Vendor bid analysis requirements should be gathered?
<--- Score

46. Is Vendor bid analysis required?
<--- Score

47. What are the dynamics of the communication plan?
<--- Score

48. How will the Vendor bid analysis team and the group measure complete success of Vendor bid analysis?
<--- Score

49. Is the scope of Vendor bid analysis defined?
<--- Score

50. How do you keep key subject matter experts in the loop?
<--- Score

51. Has a team charter been developed and communicated?
<--- Score

52. Has the Vendor bid analysis work been fairly and/or equitably divided and delegated among team members who are qualified and capable to perform the work? Has everyone contributed?
<--- Score

53. How was the 'as is' process map developed, reviewed, verified and validated?
<--- Score

54. Has everyone on the team, including the team leaders, been properly trained?
<--- Score

55. What gets examined?
<--- Score

56. What are (control) requirements for Vendor bid analysis Information?
<--- Score

57. Are there any constraints known that bear on the ability to perform Vendor bid analysis work? How is the team addressing them?
<--- Score

58. Does the scope remain the same?

<--- Score

59. How do you manage scope?
<--- Score

60. Is the current 'as is' process being followed? If not, what are the discrepancies?
<--- Score

61. Have all basic functions of Vendor bid analysis been defined?
<--- Score

62. Is there a clear Vendor bid analysis case definition?
<--- Score

63. Is the Vendor bid analysis scope manageable?
<--- Score

64. What critical content must be communicated – who, what, when, where, and how?
<--- Score

65. What happens if Vendor bid analysis's scope changes?
<--- Score

66. Does the team have regular meetings?
<--- Score

67. When is/was the Vendor bid analysis start date?
<--- Score

68. Is Vendor bid analysis linked to key stakeholder goals and objectives?
<--- Score

69. Are resources adequate for the scope?
<--- Score

70. What is out of scope?
<--- Score

71. What constraints exist that might impact the team?
<--- Score

72. How often are the team meetings?
<--- Score

73. What is the scope of the Vendor bid analysis effort?
<--- Score

74. What key stakeholder process output measure(s) does Vendor bid analysis leverage and how?
<--- Score

75. How is the team tracking and documenting its work?
<--- Score

76. What is the scope?
<--- Score

77. Will a Vendor bid analysis production readiness review be required?
<--- Score

78. Has the direction changed at all during the course of Vendor bid analysis? If so, when did it change and why?
<--- Score

79. Are task requirements clearly defined?

<--- Score

80. If substitutes have been appointed, have they been briefed on the Vendor bid analysis goals and received regular communications as to the progress to date?

<--- Score

81. Has a high-level 'as is' process map been completed, verified and validated?

<--- Score

82. Is there a critical path to deliver Vendor bid analysis results?

<--- Score

83. What is the context?

<--- Score

84. Who are the Vendor bid analysis improvement team members, including Management Leads and Coaches?

<--- Score

85. How do you manage unclear Vendor bid analysis requirements?

<--- Score

86. What is in the scope and what is not in scope?

<--- Score

87. What scope to assess?

<--- Score

88. Are customer(s) identified and segmented according to their different needs and requirements?
<--- Score

89. In what way can you redefine the criteria of choice clients have in your category in your favor?
<--- Score

90. How do you hand over Vendor bid analysis context?
<--- Score

91. Has the improvement team collected the 'voice of the customer' (obtained feedback – qualitative and quantitative)?
<--- Score

92. What are the requirements for audit information?
<--- Score

93. What baselines are required to be defined and managed?
<--- Score

94. What are the tasks and definitions?
<--- Score

95. What scope do you want your strategy to cover?
<--- Score

96. Are the Vendor bid analysis requirements testable?
<--- Score

97. Is there any additional Vendor bid analysis definition of success?
<--- Score

98. What is the worst case scenario?
<--- Score

99. What system do you use for gathering Vendor bid analysis information?
<--- Score

100. Have the customer needs been translated into specific, measurable requirements? How?
<--- Score

101. The political context: who holds power?
<--- Score

102. Is the work to date meeting requirements?
<--- Score

103. Who is gathering information?
<--- Score

104. What defines best in class?
<--- Score

105. Is there a completed, verified, and validated high-level 'as is' (not 'should be' or 'could be') stakeholder process map?
<--- Score

106. How will variation in the actual durations of each activity be dealt with to ensure that the expected Vendor bid analysis results are met?
<--- Score

107. How do you manage changes in Vendor bid analysis requirements?

<--- Score

108. Are there different segments of customers?
<--- Score

109. How are consistent Vendor bid analysis definitions important?
<--- Score

110. What are the Vendor bid analysis tasks and definitions?
<--- Score

111. What is a worst-case scenario for losses?
<--- Score

112. Is Vendor bid analysis currently on schedule according to the plan?
<--- Score

113. Has your scope been defined?
<--- Score

114. Who is gathering Vendor bid analysis information?
<--- Score

115. Is the team equipped with available and reliable resources?
<--- Score

116. How would you define the culture at your organization, how susceptible is it to Vendor bid analysis changes?
<--- Score

117. What was the context?
<--- Score

118. Do you have a Vendor bid analysis success story or case study ready to tell and share?
<--- Score

119. How do you build the right business case?
<--- Score

120. Scope of sensitive information?
<--- Score

121. Is scope creep really all bad news?
<--- Score

122. Is the improvement team aware of the different versions of a process: what they think it is vs. what it actually is vs. what it should be vs. what it could be?
<--- Score

123. What Vendor bid analysis services do you require?
<--- Score

124. Are different versions of process maps needed to account for the different types of inputs?
<--- Score

125. How do you gather the stories?
<--- Score

126. What information do you gather?
<--- Score

127. What is the definition of success?

<--- Score

128. How and when will the baselines be defined?
<--- Score

129. Are required metrics defined, what are they?
<--- Score

130. How do you think the partners involved in Vendor bid analysis would have defined success?
<--- Score

131. How do you gather Vendor bid analysis requirements?
<--- Score

132. How did the Vendor bid analysis manager receive input to the development of a Vendor bid analysis improvement plan and the estimated completion dates/times of each activity?
<--- Score

133. Is there a Vendor bid analysis management charter, including stakeholder case, problem and goal statements, scope, milestones, roles and responsibilities, communication plan?
<--- Score

134. Why are you doing Vendor bid analysis and what is the scope?
<--- Score

135. How do you gather requirements?
<--- Score

136. Will team members regularly document their

Vendor bid analysis work?
<--- Score

137. Is there a completed SIPOC representation, describing the Suppliers, Inputs, Process, Outputs, and Customers?
<--- Score

Add up total points for this section:
_____ = Total points for this section

Divided by: _____ (number of statements answered) = _____
Average score for this section

Transfer your score to the Vendor bid analysis Index at the beginning of the Self-Assessment.

CRITERION #3: MEASURE:

INTENT: Gather the correct data.
Measure the current performance and
evolution of the situation.

In my belief, the answer to this
question is clearly defined:

5 Strongly Agree

4 Agree

3 Neutral

2 Disagree

1 Strongly Disagree

1. How are measurements made?
<--- Score

2. Is there an opportunity to verify requirements?
<--- Score

3. How will you measure success?
<--- Score

4. What tests verify requirements?

<--- Score

5. What can be used to verify compliance?

<--- Score

6. Which Vendor bid analysis impacts are significant?

<--- Score

7. Have you made assumptions about the shape of the future, particularly its impact on your customers and competitors?

<--- Score

8. How do you measure success?

<--- Score

9. What potential environmental factors impact the Vendor bid analysis effort?

<--- Score

10. Does a Vendor bid analysis quantification method exist?

<--- Score

11. How do you verify performance?

<--- Score

12. Who is involved in verifying compliance?

<--- Score

13. What is an unallowable cost?

<--- Score

14. How is progress measured?

<--- Score

15. How is the value delivered by Vendor bid analysis being measured?
<--- Score

16. What are the costs of reform?
<--- Score

17. What do you measure and why?
<--- Score

18. Are you able to realize any cost savings?
<--- Score

19. Did you tackle the cause or the symptom?
<--- Score

20. Was a business case (cost/benefit) developed?
<--- Score

21. Do you have a flow diagram of what happens?
<--- Score

22. What could cause you to change course?
<--- Score

23. How will effects be measured?
<--- Score

24. What are the operational costs after Vendor bid analysis deployment?
<--- Score

25. What evidence is there and what is measured?
<--- Score

26. How will costs be allocated?
<--- Score

27. Has a cost center been established?
<--- Score

28. Does the Vendor bid analysis task fit the client's priorities?
<--- Score

29. How do you verify if Vendor bid analysis is built right?
<--- Score

30. What are allowable costs?
<--- Score

31. How do you measure lifecycle phases?
<--- Score

32. How do you verify the authenticity of the data and information used?
<--- Score

33. What are your customers expectations and measures?
<--- Score

34. What would be a real cause for concern?
<--- Score

35. What methods are feasible and acceptable to estimate the impact of reforms?
<--- Score

36. How do you measure variability?

<--- Score

37. How can you manage cost down?
<--- Score

38. How will success or failure be measured?
<--- Score

39. Are you taking your company in the direction of better and revenue or cheaper and cost?
<--- Score

40. What would it cost to replace your technology?
<--- Score

41. What causes extra work or rework?
<--- Score

42. Are actual costs in line with budgeted costs?
<--- Score

43. What users will be impacted?
<--- Score

44. What are the costs and benefits?
<--- Score

45. What are the strategic priorities for this year?
<--- Score

46. How do you verify and develop ideas and innovations?
<--- Score

47. Is the solution cost-effective?
<--- Score

48. What are the costs?
<--- Score

49. What are the costs of delaying Vendor bid analysis action?
<--- Score

50. What is your Vendor bid analysis quality cost segregation study?
<--- Score

51. How are costs allocated?
<--- Score

52. What disadvantage does this cause for the user?
<--- Score

53. Will Vendor bid analysis have an impact on current business continuity, disaster recovery processes and/ or infrastructure?
<--- Score

54. Have design-to-cost goals been established?
<--- Score

55. Are missed Vendor bid analysis opportunities costing your organization money?
<--- Score

56. Where can you go to verify the info?
<--- Score

57. How do you aggregate measures across priorities?
<--- Score

58. Do you have an issue in getting priority?
<--- Score

59. How much does it cost?
<--- Score

60. Which costs should be taken into account?
<--- Score

61. What could cause delays in the schedule?
<--- Score

62. How do you verify the Vendor bid analysis requirements quality?
<--- Score

63. What relevant entities could be measured?
<--- Score

64. Are the Vendor bid analysis benefits worth its costs?
<--- Score

65. How frequently do you track Vendor bid analysis measures?
<--- Score

66. What details are required of the Vendor bid analysis cost structure?
<--- Score

67. Are there competing Vendor bid analysis priorities?
<--- Score

68. When should you bother with diagrams?

<--- Score

69. When a disaster occurs, who gets priority?
<--- Score

70. What causes investor action?
<--- Score

71. How do your measurements capture actionable Vendor bid analysis information for use in exceeding your customers expectations and securing your customers engagement?
<--- Score

72. What causes mismanagement?
<--- Score

73. How can you reduce costs?
<--- Score

74. What are hidden Vendor bid analysis quality costs?
<--- Score

75. How do you measure efficient delivery of Vendor bid analysis services?
<--- Score

76. Are indirect costs charged to the Vendor bid analysis program?
<--- Score

77. Why do the measurements/indicators matter?
<--- Score

78. What are the Vendor bid analysis key cost drivers?
<--- Score

79. What is the cost of rework?
<--- Score

80. How do you control the overall costs of your work processes?
<--- Score

81. How can you measure Vendor bid analysis in a systematic way?
<--- Score

82. What causes innovation to fail or succeed in your organization?
<--- Score

83. Is the cost worth the Vendor bid analysis effort ?
<--- Score

84. What is the total fixed cost?
<--- Score

85. What is your decision requirements diagram?
<--- Score

86. What happens if cost savings do not materialize?
<--- Score

87. What are your primary costs, revenues, assets?
<--- Score

88. What measurements are being captured?
<--- Score

89. How long to keep data and how to manage retention costs?

<--- Score

90. What drives O&M cost?
<--- Score

91. What are the Vendor bid analysis investment costs?
<--- Score

92. What are the uncertainties surrounding estimates of impact?
<--- Score

93. Which measures and indicators matter?
<--- Score

94. What are the estimated costs of proposed changes?
<--- Score

95. What are the current costs of the Vendor bid analysis process?
<--- Score

96. How do you verify Vendor bid analysis completeness and accuracy?
<--- Score

97. Among the Vendor bid analysis product and service cost to be estimated, which is considered hardest to estimate?
<--- Score

98. What measurements are possible, practicable and meaningful?
<--- Score

99. What does your operating model cost?
<--- Score

100. What are your operating costs?
<--- Score

101. What is the Vendor bid analysis business impact?
<--- Score

102. What is the root cause(s) of the problem?
<--- Score

103. Do you verify that corrective actions were taken?
<--- Score

104. What do people want to verify?
<--- Score

105. Do you have any cost Vendor bid analysis limitation requirements?
<--- Score

106. Do you effectively measure and reward individual and team performance?
<--- Score

107. What harm might be caused?
<--- Score

108. What are you verifying?
<--- Score

109. Are supply costs steady or fluctuating?
<--- Score

110. How will measures be used to manage and adapt?
<--- Score

111. Are the units of measure consistent?
<--- Score

112. How do you prevent mis-estimating cost?
<--- Score

113. Do you aggressively reward and promote the people who have the biggest impact on creating excellent Vendor bid analysis services/products?
<--- Score

114. When are costs are incurred?
<--- Score

115. Are Vendor bid analysis vulnerabilities categorized and prioritized?
<--- Score

116. Where is it measured?
<--- Score

117. How is performance measured?
<--- Score

118. Are there measurements based on task performance?
<--- Score

119. Are there any easy-to-implement alternatives to Vendor bid analysis? Sometimes other solutions are available that do not require the cost implications of a full-blown project?

<--- Score

120. Why do you expend time and effort to implement measurement, for whom?
<--- Score

121. How will your organization measure success?
<--- Score

122. What is the total cost related to deploying Vendor bid analysis, including any consulting or professional services?
<--- Score

123. What are the types and number of measures to use?
<--- Score

124. Have you included everything in your Vendor bid analysis cost models?
<--- Score

125. How can you measure the performance?
<--- Score

126. Where is the cost?
<--- Score

127. Do the benefits outweigh the costs?
<--- Score

128. Does management have the right priorities among projects?
<--- Score

129. Is it possible to estimate the impact of

unanticipated complexity such as wrong or failed assumptions, feedback, etcetera on proposed reforms?

<--- Score

130. How do you verify and validate the Vendor bid analysis data?

<--- Score

131. What are your key Vendor bid analysis organizational performance measures, including key short and longer-term financial measures?

<--- Score

132. How can a Vendor bid analysis test verify your ideas or assumptions?

<--- Score

133. At what cost?

<--- Score

134. Who pays the cost?

<--- Score

135. What does losing customers cost your organization?

<--- Score

136. How do you verify your resources?

<--- Score

137. How can you reduce the costs of obtaining inputs?

<--- Score

138. What is the cause of any Vendor bid analysis

gaps?
<--- Score

139. How sensitive must the Vendor bid analysis strategy be to cost?
<--- Score

Add up total points for this section:
_____ = Total points for this section

Divided by: _____ (number of statements answered) = _____
Average score for this section

Transfer your score to the Vendor bid analysis Index at the beginning of the Self-Assessment.

CRITERION #4: ANALYZE:

INTENT: Analyze causes, assumptions and hypotheses.

In my belief, the answer to this question is clearly defined:

5 Strongly Agree

4 Agree

3 Neutral

2 Disagree

1 Strongly Disagree

1. Do quality systems drive continuous improvement?
<--- Score

2. How much data can be collected in the given timeframe?
<--- Score

3. Is there an established change management process?
<--- Score

4. What are the disruptive Vendor bid analysis technologies that enable your organization to radically change your business processes?
<--- Score

5. How do you identify specific Vendor bid analysis investment opportunities and emerging trends?
<--- Score

6. How does the organization define, manage, and improve its Vendor bid analysis processes?
<--- Score

7. Has data output been validated?
<--- Score

8. Which Vendor bid analysis data should be retained?
<--- Score

9. Where can you get qualified talent today?
<--- Score

10. Is the gap/opportunity displayed and communicated in financial terms?
<--- Score

11. Can you add value to the current Vendor bid analysis decision-making process (largely qualitative) by incorporating uncertainty modeling (more quantitative)?
<--- Score

12. What do you need to qualify?
<--- Score

13. What output to create?
<--- Score

14. Do your contracts/agreements contain data security obligations?
<--- Score

15. What Vendor bid analysis data will be collected?
<--- Score

16. Is there a strict change management process?
<--- Score

17. What training and qualifications will you need?
<--- Score

18. What qualifications do Vendor bid analysis leaders need?
<--- Score

19. How has the Vendor bid analysis data been gathered?
<--- Score

20. How do you measure the operational performance of your key work systems and processes, including productivity, cycle time, and other appropriate measures of process effectiveness, efficiency, and innovation?
<--- Score

21. Were any designed experiments used to generate additional insight into the data analysis?
<--- Score

22. Was a cause-and-effect diagram used to explore

the different types of causes (or sources of variation)?
<--- Score

23. How difficult is it to qualify what Vendor bid analysis ROI is?
<--- Score

24. What controls do you have in place to protect data?
<--- Score

25. What tools were used to narrow the list of possible causes?
<--- Score

26. Do staff qualifications match your project?
<--- Score

27. How is the way you as the leader think and process information affecting your organizational culture?
<--- Score

28. Think about some of the processes you undertake within your organization, which do you own?
<--- Score

29. What other jobs or tasks affect the performance of the steps in the Vendor bid analysis process?
<--- Score

30. How many input/output points does it require?
<--- Score

31. What resources go in to get the desired output?
<--- Score

32. Where is Vendor bid analysis data gathered?
<--- Score

33. What methods do you use to gather Vendor bid analysis data?
<--- Score

34. Were Pareto charts (or similar) used to portray the 'heavy hitters' (or key sources of variation)?
<--- Score

35. When should a process be art not science?
<--- Score

36. Do you, as a leader, bounce back quickly from setbacks?
<--- Score

37. Think about the functions involved in your Vendor bid analysis project, what processes flow from these functions?
<--- Score

38. How is data used for program management and improvement?
<--- Score

39. Who is involved with workflow mapping?
<--- Score

40. An organizationally feasible system request is one that considers the mission, goals and objectives of the organization, key questions are: is the Vendor bid analysis solution request practical and will it solve a problem or take advantage of an opportunity to achieve company goals?

<--- Score

41. Was a detailed process map created to amplify critical steps of the 'as is' stakeholder process?
<--- Score

42. What systems/processes must you excel at?
<--- Score

43. A compounding model resolution with available relevant data can often provide insight towards a solution methodology; which Vendor bid analysis models, tools and techniques are necessary?
<--- Score

44. Is the suppliers process defined and controlled?
<--- Score

45. Is pre-qualification of suppliers carried out?
<--- Score

46. Identify an operational issue in your organization, for example, could a particular task be done more quickly or more efficiently by Vendor bid analysis?
<--- Score

47. How will the change process be managed?
<--- Score

48. Do several people in different organizational units assist with the Vendor bid analysis process?
<--- Score

49. What Vendor bid analysis metrics are outputs of the process?
<--- Score

50. What qualifications are necessary?
<--- Score

51. How is the Vendor bid analysis Value Stream Mapping managed?
<--- Score

52. What data is gathered?
<--- Score

53. What is the cost of poor quality as supported by the team's analysis?
<--- Score

54. What are your current levels and trends in key Vendor bid analysis measures or indicators of product and process performance that are important to and directly serve your customers?
<--- Score

55. What kind of crime could a potential new hire have committed that would not only not disqualify him/her from being hired by your organization, but would actually indicate that he/she might be a particularly good fit?
<--- Score

56. What quality tools were used to get through the analyze phase?
<--- Score

57. Who qualifies to gain access to data?
<--- Score

58. Has an output goal been set?

<--- Score

59. What is the oversight process?
<--- Score

60. Are Vendor bid analysis changes recognized early enough to be approved through the regular process?
<--- Score

61. What, related to, Vendor bid analysis processes does your organization outsource?
<--- Score

62. Do your leaders quickly bounce back from setbacks?
<--- Score

63. Who will gather what data?
<--- Score

64. What are your current levels and trends in key measures or indicators of Vendor bid analysis product and process performance that are important to and directly serve your customers? How do these results compare with the performance of your competitors and other organizations with similar offerings?
<--- Score

65. What successful thing are you doing today that may be blinding you to new growth opportunities?
<--- Score

66. What are the processes for audit reporting and management?
<--- Score

67. Should you invest in industry-recognized qualifications?
<--- Score

68. What does the data say about the performance of the stakeholder process?
<--- Score

69. What is the output?
<--- Score

70. How is the data gathered?
<--- Score

71. Are gaps between current performance and the goal performance identified?
<--- Score

72. What qualifies as competition?
<--- Score

73. What is the complexity of the output produced?
<--- Score

74. What are the revised rough estimates of the financial savings/opportunity for Vendor bid analysis improvements?
<--- Score

75. What Vendor bid analysis data should be managed?
<--- Score

76. Is the required Vendor bid analysis data gathered?
<--- Score

77. How do you use Vendor bid analysis data and information to support organizational decision making and innovation?
<--- Score

78. How will the data be checked for quality?
<--- Score

79. Does an RFP provide you with an opportunity to expand into new areas or acquire a new type of expertise?
<--- Score

80. What were the crucial 'moments of truth' on the process map?
<--- Score

81. How do mission and objectives affect the Vendor bid analysis processes of your organization?
<--- Score

82. Is the Vendor bid analysis process severely broken such that a re-design is necessary?
<--- Score

83. How do you implement and manage your work processes to ensure that they meet design requirements?
<--- Score

84. What data do you need to collect?
<--- Score

85. How do you define collaboration and team output?
<--- Score

86. How can risk management be tied procedurally to process elements?
<--- Score

87. What were the financial benefits resulting from any 'ground fruit or low-hanging fruit' (quick fixes)?
<--- Score

88. How do you ensure that the Vendor bid analysis opportunity is realistic?
<--- Score

89. Have any additional benefits been identified that will result from closing all or most of the gaps?
<--- Score

90. What tools were used to generate the list of possible causes?
<--- Score

91. Are your outputs consistent?
<--- Score

92. Are all team members qualified for all tasks?
<--- Score

93. What internal processes need improvement?
<--- Score

94. What did the team gain from developing a sub-process map?
<--- Score

95. Are you missing Vendor bid analysis opportunities?

<--- Score

96. How will the Vendor bid analysis data be captured?
<--- Score

97. What are evaluation criteria for the output?
<--- Score

98. Have the problem and goal statements been updated to reflect the additional knowledge gained from the analyze phase?
<--- Score

99. Were there any improvement opportunities identified from the process analysis?
<--- Score

100. What is your organizations system for selecting qualified vendors?
<--- Score

101. What is your organizations process which leads to recognition of value generation?
<--- Score

102. What are the Vendor bid analysis design outputs?
<--- Score

103. How do your work systems and key work processes relate to and capitalize on your core competencies?
<--- Score

104. Did any value-added analysis or 'lean thinking' take place to identify some of the gaps shown on the

'as is' process map?
<--- Score

105. Who is involved in the management review process?
<--- Score

106. How was the detailed process map generated, verified, and validated?
<--- Score

107. Are all staff in core Vendor bid analysis subjects Highly Qualified?
<--- Score

108. Have you defined which data is gathered how?
<--- Score

109. Is the performance gap determined?
<--- Score

110. What qualifications and skills do you need?
<--- Score

111. What are your best practices for minimizing Vendor bid analysis project risk, while demonstrating incremental value and quick wins throughout the Vendor bid analysis project lifecycle?
<--- Score

112. What conclusions were drawn from the team's data collection and analysis? How did the team reach these conclusions?
<--- Score

113. What is the Vendor bid analysis Driver?

<--- Score

114. Who owns what data?
<--- Score

115. What are the necessary qualifications?
<--- Score

116. How are outputs preserved and protected?
<--- Score

117. Who gets your output?
<--- Score

118. What information qualified as important?
<--- Score

119. How is Vendor bid analysis data gathered?
<--- Score

120. What will drive Vendor bid analysis change?
<--- Score

121. What process improvements will be needed?
<--- Score

122. What are your key performance measures or indicators and in-process measures for the control and improvement of your Vendor bid analysis processes?
<--- Score

123. What types of data do your Vendor bid analysis indicators require?
<--- Score

124. Is there any way to speed up the process?
<--- Score

125. Do your employees have the opportunity to do what they do best everyday?
<--- Score

126. Did any additional data need to be collected?
<--- Score

127. What process should you select for improvement?
<--- Score

128. What Vendor bid analysis data should be collected?
<--- Score

129. How often will data be collected for measures?
<--- Score

130. Is the final output clearly identified?
<--- Score

131. What are the personnel training and qualifications required?
<--- Score

132. Is data and process analysis, root cause analysis and quantifying the gap/opportunity in place?
<--- Score

133. Where is the data coming from to measure compliance?
<--- Score

134. How will corresponding data be collected?
<--- Score

135. What are the best opportunities for value improvement?
<--- Score

136. Do you have the authority to produce the output?
<--- Score

137. Who will facilitate the team and process?
<--- Score

138. What are the Vendor bid analysis business drivers?
<--- Score

Add up total points for this section:
_ _ _ _ _ = Total points for this section

Divided by: _ _ _ _ _ _ (number of statements answered) = _ _ _ _ _ _
Average score for this section

Transfer your score to the Vendor bid analysis Index at the beginning of the Self-Assessment.

CRITERION #5: IMPROVE:

INTENT: Develop a practical solution.
Innovate, establish and test the
solution and to measure the results.

In my belief, the answer to this
question is clearly defined:

5 Strongly Agree

4 Agree

3 Neutral

2 Disagree

1 Strongly Disagree

1. Who makes the Vendor bid analysis decisions in your organization?
<--- Score

2. What strategies for Vendor bid analysis improvement are successful?
<--- Score

3. Explorations of the frontiers of Vendor bid analysis

will help you build influence, improve Vendor bid analysis, optimize decision making, and sustain change, what is your approach?
<--- Score

4. How do you link measurement and risk?
<--- Score

5. How do you improve your likelihood of success ?
<--- Score

6. How does your organization evaluate strategic Vendor bid analysis success?
<--- Score

7. Was a pilot designed for the proposed solution(s)?
<--- Score

8. Which Vendor bid analysis solution is appropriate?
<--- Score

9. How will you know when its improved?
<--- Score

10. What are the Vendor bid analysis security risks?
<--- Score

11. Have you identified breakpoints and/or risk tolerances that will trigger broad consideration of a potential need for intervention or modification of strategy?
<--- Score

12. Is Vendor bid analysis documentation maintained?
<--- Score

13. Who are the key stakeholders for the Vendor bid analysis evaluation?
<--- Score

14. How do you manage Vendor bid analysis risk?
<--- Score

15. Who are the people involved in developing and implementing Vendor bid analysis?
<--- Score

16. Is the Vendor bid analysis documentation thorough?
<--- Score

17. Who will be using the results of the measurement activities?
<--- Score

18. Who will be responsible for documenting the Vendor bid analysis requirements in detail?
<--- Score

19. Who manages Vendor bid analysis risk?
<--- Score

20. Can you integrate quality management and risk management?
<--- Score

21. What are your current levels and trends in key measures or indicators of workforce and leader development?
<--- Score

22. What should a proof of concept or pilot

accomplish?
<--- Score

23. What are the concrete Vendor bid analysis results?
<--- Score

24. What lessons, if any, from a pilot were incorporated into the design of the full-scale solution?
<--- Score

25. Is any Vendor bid analysis documentation required?
<--- Score

26. Are decisions made in a timely manner?
<--- Score

27. What practices helps your organization to develop its capacity to recognize patterns?
<--- Score

28. Have you achieved Vendor bid analysis improvements?
<--- Score

29. What are the expected Vendor bid analysis results?
<--- Score

30. How do you mitigate Vendor bid analysis risk?
<--- Score

31. Do you cover the five essential competencies: Communication, Collaboration,Innovation, Adaptability, and Leadership that improve an organizations ability to leverage the new Vendor bid analysis in a volatile global economy?

<--- Score

32. To what extent does management recognize Vendor bid analysis as a tool to increase the results?
<--- Score

33. Is there any other Vendor bid analysis solution?
<--- Score

34. What resources are required for the improvement efforts?
<--- Score

35. How do you measure improved Vendor bid analysis service perception, and satisfaction?
<--- Score

36. How do you measure risk?
<--- Score

37. What risks do you need to manage?
<--- Score

38. Does a good decision guarantee a good outcome?
<--- Score

39. How does the team improve its work?
<--- Score

40. Is the solution technically practical?
<--- Score

41. How do you manage and improve your Vendor bid analysis work systems to deliver customer value and achieve organizational success and sustainability?
<--- Score

42. Who are the Vendor bid analysis decision makers?
<--- Score

43. Who should make the Vendor bid analysis decisions?
<--- Score

44. What improvements have been achieved?
<--- Score

45. Was a Vendor bid analysis charter developed?
<--- Score

46. What are the implications of the one critical Vendor bid analysis decision 10 minutes, 10 months, and 10 years from now?
<--- Score

47. What current systems have to be understood and/or changed?
<--- Score

48. How will you measure the results?
<--- Score

49. What tools were used to tap into the creativity and encourage 'outside the box' thinking?
<--- Score

50. Were any criteria developed to assist the team in testing and evaluating potential solutions?
<--- Score

51. Do you have the optimal project management team structure?

<--- Score

52. What tools were most useful during the improve phase?
<--- Score

53. How can the phases of Vendor bid analysis development be identified?
<--- Score

54. What assumptions are made about the solution and approach?
<--- Score

55. When you map the key players in your own work and the types/domains of relationships with them, which relationships do you find easy and which challenging, and why?
<--- Score

56. What are the affordable Vendor bid analysis risks?
<--- Score

57. How do you decide how much to remunerate an employee?
<--- Score

58. How is knowledge sharing about risk management improved?
<--- Score

59. Would you develop a Vendor bid analysis Communication Strategy?
<--- Score

60. Are risk management tasks balanced centrally and

locally?
<--- Score

61. What attendant changes will need to be made to ensure that the solution is successful?
<--- Score

62. What went well, what should change, what can improve?
<--- Score

63. How can you better manage risk?
<--- Score

64. Risk factors: what are the characteristics of Vendor bid analysis that make it risky?
<--- Score

65. Does the goal represent a desired result that can be measured?
<--- Score

66. Who will be responsible for making the decisions to include or exclude requested changes once Vendor bid analysis is underway?
<--- Score

67. Is there a high likelihood that any recommendations will achieve their intended results?
<--- Score

68. What is Vendor bid analysis risk?
<--- Score

69. What is the risk?
<--- Score

70. Are you assessing Vendor bid analysis and risk?
<--- Score

71. What communications are necessary to support the implementation of the solution?
<--- Score

72. What is the magnitude of the improvements?
<--- Score

73. Is supporting Vendor bid analysis documentation required?
<--- Score

74. Where do you need Vendor bid analysis improvement?
<--- Score

75. Risk events: what are the things that could go wrong?
<--- Score

76. Do you need to do a usability evaluation?
<--- Score

77. How will you recognize and celebrate results?
<--- Score

78. Do vendor agreements bring new compliance risk ?
<--- Score

79. How risky is your organization?
<--- Score

80. How will you know that you have improved?
<--- Score

81. Who manages supplier risk management in your organization?
<--- Score

82. Is the measure of success for Vendor bid analysis understandable to a variety of people?
<--- Score

83. How significant is the improvement in the eyes of the end user?
<--- Score

84. How can you improve performance?
<--- Score

85. Is the Vendor bid analysis risk managed?
<--- Score

86. Can you identify any significant risks or exposures to Vendor bid analysis third- parties (vendors, service providers, alliance partners etc) that concern you?
<--- Score

87. For estimation problems, how do you develop an estimation statement?
<--- Score

88. Are events managed to resolution?
<--- Score

89. What area needs the greatest improvement?
<--- Score

90. How do you measure progress and evaluate training effectiveness?
<--- Score

91. Are the key business and technology risks being managed?
<--- Score

92. Will the controls trigger any other risks?
<--- Score

93. Who will evaluate an RFP responses?
<--- Score

94. What error proofing will be done to address some of the discrepancies observed in the 'as is' process?
<--- Score

95. How can skill-level changes improve Vendor bid analysis?
<--- Score

96. How do the Vendor bid analysis results compare with the performance of your competitors and other organizations with similar offerings?
<--- Score

97. What do you want to improve?
<--- Score

98. How is continuous improvement applied to risk management?
<--- Score

99. How do you keep improving Vendor bid analysis?
<--- Score

100. Are the most efficient solutions problem-specific?
<--- Score

101. Who do you report Vendor bid analysis results to?
<--- Score

102. What criteria will you use to assess your Vendor bid analysis risks?
<--- Score

103. Is the Vendor bid analysis solution sustainable?
<--- Score

104. How do you deal with Vendor bid analysis risk?
<--- Score

105. What tools do you use once you have decided on a Vendor bid analysis strategy and more importantly how do you choose?
<--- Score

106. Is the scope clearly documented?
<--- Score

107. How are Vendor bid analysis risks managed?
<--- Score

108. Do those selected for the Vendor bid analysis team have a good general understanding of what Vendor bid analysis is all about?
<--- Score

109. For decision problems, how do you develop a decision statement?
<--- Score

110. Where do the Vendor bid analysis decisions reside?
<--- Score

111. What can you do to improve?
<--- Score

112. Vendor bid analysis risk decisions: whose call Is It?
<--- Score

113. What were the criteria for evaluating a Vendor bid analysis pilot?
<--- Score

114. If you could go back in time five years, what decision would you make differently? What is your best guess as to what decision you're making today you might regret five years from now?
<--- Score

115. What is the Vendor bid analysis's sustainability risk?
<--- Score

116. At what point will vulnerability assessments be performed once Vendor bid analysis is put into production (e.g., ongoing Risk Management after implementation)?
<--- Score

117. How do you go about comparing Vendor bid analysis approaches/solutions?
<--- Score

118. What alternative responses are available to

manage risk?
<--- Score

119. What is Vendor bid analysis's impact on utilizing the best solution(s)?
<--- Score

120. How do you define the solutions' scope?
<--- Score

121. In the past few months, what is the smallest change you have made that has had the biggest positive result? What was it about that small change that produced the large return?
<--- Score

122. Are the risks fully understood, reasonable and manageable?
<--- Score

123. What actually has to improve and by how much?
<--- Score

124. Are procedures documented for managing Vendor bid analysis risks?
<--- Score

125. Is there a small-scale pilot for proposed improvement(s)? What conclusions were drawn from the outcomes of a pilot?
<--- Score

126. What Vendor bid analysis improvements can be made?
<--- Score

127. Who are the Vendor bid analysis decision-makers?
<--- Score

128. How do you improve Vendor bid analysis service perception, and satisfaction?
<--- Score

129. Who controls the risk?
<--- Score

130. Who controls key decisions that will be made?
<--- Score

131. Are risk triggers captured?
<--- Score

132. What is the implementation plan?
<--- Score

133. Is risk periodically assessed?
<--- Score

134. What were the underlying assumptions on the cost-benefit analysis?
<--- Score

135. What to do with the results or outcomes of measurements?
<--- Score

136. What tools were used to evaluate the potential solutions?
<--- Score

137. What is the team's contingency plan for potential

problems occurring in implementation?
<--- Score

138. How scalable is your Vendor bid analysis solution?
<--- Score

139. How do you improve productivity?
<--- Score

140. What does the 'should be' process map/design look like?
<--- Score

141. Why improve in the first place?
<--- Score

142. What needs improvement? Why?
<--- Score

Add up total points for this section:
_ _ _ _ _ = Total points for this section

Divided by: _ _ _ _ _ _ (number of statements answered) = _ _ _ _ _ _
Average score for this section

Transfer your score to the Vendor bid analysis Index at the beginning of the Self-Assessment.

CRITERION #6: CONTROL:

INTENT: Implement the practical solution. Maintain the performance and correct possible complications.

In my belief, the answer to this question is clearly defined:

5 Strongly Agree

4 Agree

3 Neutral

2 Disagree

1 Strongly Disagree

1. Does the Vendor bid analysis performance meet the customer's requirements?
<--- Score

2. Who is going to spread your message?
<--- Score

3. Who has control over resources?
<--- Score

4. Will existing staff require re-training, for example, to learn new business processes?
<--- Score

5. Are suggested corrective/restorative actions indicated on the response plan for known causes to problems that might surface?
<--- Score

6. Are the planned controls working?
<--- Score

7. Does a troubleshooting guide exist or is it needed?
<--- Score

8. Against what alternative is success being measured?
<--- Score

9. Is there a Vendor bid analysis Communication plan covering who needs to get what information when?
<--- Score

10. Will your goals reflect your program budget?
<--- Score

11. Is there an action plan in case of emergencies?
<--- Score

12. Who controls critical resources?
<--- Score

13. Do the Vendor bid analysis decisions you make today help people and the planet tomorrow?
<--- Score

14. How will Vendor bid analysis decisions be made and monitored?

<--- Score

15. What is the control/monitoring plan?

<--- Score

16. What are your results for key measures or indicators of the accomplishment of your Vendor bid analysis strategy and action plans, including building and strengthening core competencies?

<--- Score

17. Who will be in control?

<--- Score

18. How is Vendor bid analysis project cost planned, managed, monitored?

<--- Score

19. What do you measure to verify effectiveness gains?

<--- Score

20. How will input, process, and output variables be checked to detect for sub-optimal conditions?

<--- Score

21. What are the known security controls?

<--- Score

22. What is the standard for acceptable Vendor bid analysis performance?

<--- Score

23. Are new process steps, standards, and documentation ingrained into normal operations?
<--- Score

24. What do you stand for--and what are you against?
<--- Score

25. How likely is the current Vendor bid analysis plan to come in on schedule or on budget?
<--- Score

26. What can you control?
<--- Score

27. Can you adapt and adjust to changing Vendor bid analysis situations?
<--- Score

28. Who is the Vendor bid analysis process owner?
<--- Score

29. Are there documented procedures?
<--- Score

30. How is change control managed?
<--- Score

31. Is reporting being used or needed?
<--- Score

32. Is there a recommended audit plan for routine surveillance inspections of Vendor bid analysis's gains?
<--- Score

33. How will new or emerging customer needs/

requirements be checked/communicated to orient the process toward meeting the new specifications and continually reducing variation?
<--- Score

34. What is your plan to assess your security risks?
<--- Score

35. What is the best design framework for Vendor bid analysis organization now that, in a post industrial-age if the top-down, command and control model is no longer relevant?
<--- Score

36. How do your controls stack up?
<--- Score

37. How will report readings be checked to effectively monitor performance?
<--- Score

38. Implementation Planning: is a pilot needed to test the changes before a full roll out occurs?
<--- Score

39. Is the Vendor bid analysis test/monitoring cost justified?
<--- Score

40. Do you monitor the effectiveness of your Vendor bid analysis activities?
<--- Score

41. Does the response plan contain a definite closed loop continual improvement scheme (e.g., plan-do-check-act)?

<--- Score

42. What other areas of the group might benefit from the Vendor bid analysis team's improvements, knowledge, and learning?
<--- Score

43. What do your reports reflect?
<--- Score

44. In the case of a Vendor bid analysis project, the criteria for the audit derive from implementation objectives, an audit of a Vendor bid analysis project involves assessing whether the recommendations outlined for implementation have been met, can you track that any Vendor bid analysis project is implemented as planned, and is it working?
<--- Score

45. Is there a control plan in place for sustaining improvements (short and long-term)?
<--- Score

46. How do you plan for the cost of succession?
<--- Score

47. How do controls support value?
<--- Score

48. How can you best use all of your knowledge repositories to enhance learning and sharing?
<--- Score

49. Is a response plan established and deployed?
<--- Score

50. What is the recommended frequency of auditing?
<--- Score

51. How do you monitor usage and cost?
<--- Score

52. Is there a transfer of ownership and knowledge to process owner and process team tasked with the responsibilities.
<--- Score

53. Do you monitor the Vendor bid analysis decisions made and fine tune them as they evolve?
<--- Score

54. Are operating procedures consistent?
<--- Score

55. What other systems, operations, processes, and infrastructures (hiring practices, staffing, training, incentives/rewards, metrics/dashboards/scorecards, etc.) need updates, additions, changes, or deletions in order to facilitate knowledge transfer and improvements?
<--- Score

56. Will any special training be provided for results interpretation?
<--- Score

57. Act/Adjust: What Do you Need to Do Differently?
<--- Score

58. Is knowledge gained on process shared and institutionalized?
<--- Score

59. Is there a documented and implemented monitoring plan?
<--- Score

60. Have new or revised work instructions resulted?
<--- Score

61. How do you select, collect, align, and integrate Vendor bid analysis data and information for tracking daily operations and overall organizational performance, including progress relative to strategic objectives and action plans?
<--- Score

62. Are pertinent alerts monitored, analyzed and distributed to appropriate personnel?
<--- Score

63. What adjustments to the strategies are needed?
<--- Score

64. Is there documentation that will support the successful operation of the improvement?
<--- Score

65. How will you measure your QA plan's effectiveness?
<--- Score

66. What are the performance and scale of the Vendor bid analysis tools?
<--- Score

67. How do you encourage people to take control and responsibility?

<--- Score

68. Is a response plan in place for when the input, process, or output measures indicate an 'out-of-control' condition?
<--- Score

69. How will the process owner and team be able to hold the gains?
<--- Score

70. Does Vendor bid analysis appropriately measure and monitor risk?
<--- Score

71. Has the improved process and its steps been standardized?
<--- Score

72. Can support from partners be adjusted?
<--- Score

73. What are the critical parameters to watch?
<--- Score

74. What is your theory of human motivation, and how does your compensation plan fit with that view?
<--- Score

75. Is there a standardized process?
<--- Score

76. How will the day-to-day responsibilities for monitoring and continual improvement be transferred from the improvement team to the process owner?

<--- Score

77. Is new knowledge gained imbedded in the response plan?
<--- Score

78. Will the team be available to assist members in planning investigations?
<--- Score

79. What key inputs and outputs are being measured on an ongoing basis?
<--- Score

80. What should the next improvement project be that is related to Vendor bid analysis?
<--- Score

81. What should you measure to verify efficiency gains?
<--- Score

82. Are controls in place and consistently applied?
<--- Score

83. Has the Vendor bid analysis value of standards been quantified?
<--- Score

84. How might the group capture best practices and lessons learned so as to leverage improvements?
<--- Score

85. Do the viable solutions scale to future needs?
<--- Score

86. You may have created your quality measures at a time when you lacked resources, technology wasn't up to the required standard, or low service levels were the industry norm. Have those circumstances changed?
<--- Score

87. How do you spread information?
<--- Score

88. Are the Vendor bid analysis standards challenging?
<--- Score

89. Who sets the Vendor bid analysis standards?
<--- Score

90. Are documented procedures clear and easy to follow for the operators?
<--- Score

91. Are you measuring, monitoring and predicting Vendor bid analysis activities to optimize operations and profitability, and enhancing outcomes?
<--- Score

92. What are you attempting to measure/monitor?
<--- Score

93. How do senior leaders actions reflect a commitment to the organizations Vendor bid analysis values?
<--- Score

94. How widespread is its use?
<--- Score

95. What are customers monitoring?
<--- Score

96. How do you establish and deploy modified action plans if circumstances require a shift in plans and rapid execution of new plans?
<--- Score

97. Does job training on the documented procedures need to be part of the process team's education and training?
<--- Score

98. What quality tools were useful in the control phase?
<--- Score

99. How will the process owner verify improvement in present and future sigma levels, process capabilities?
<--- Score

Add up total points for this section:
_ _ _ _ _ = Total points for this section

Divided by: _ _ _ _ _ _ (number of statements answered) = _ _ _ _ _ _
Average score for this section

Transfer your score to the Vendor bid analysis Index at the beginning of the Self-Assessment.

CRITERION #7: SUSTAIN:

INTENT: Retain the benefits.

In my belief, the answer to this question is clearly defined:

5 Strongly Agree

4 Agree

3 Neutral

2 Disagree

1 Strongly Disagree

1. What is your Vendor bid analysis strategy?
<--- Score

2. Are you using a design thinking approach and integrating Innovation, Vendor bid analysis Experience, and Brand Value?
<--- Score

3. Are you satisfied with your current role? If not, what is missing from it?
<--- Score

4. Were lessons learned captured and communicated?
<--- Score

5. How do you maintain Vendor bid analysis's Integrity?
<--- Score

6. Which models, tools and techniques are necessary?
<--- Score

7. What are the rules and assumptions your industry operates under? What if the opposite were true?
<--- Score

8. What unique value proposition (UVP) do you offer?
<--- Score

9. What relationships among Vendor bid analysis trends do you perceive?
<--- Score

10. How do you ensure that implementations of Vendor bid analysis products are done in a way that ensures safety?
<--- Score

11. What have been your experiences in defining long range Vendor bid analysis goals?
<--- Score

12. Are new benefits received and understood?
<--- Score

13. What are the key enablers to make this Vendor bid analysis move?

<--- Score

14. Who are the key stakeholders?
<--- Score

15. Who do you think the world wants your organization to be?
<--- Score

16. Are the assumptions believable and achievable?
<--- Score

17. How do you listen to customers to obtain actionable information?
<--- Score

18. What is something you believe that nearly no one agrees with you on?
<--- Score

19. How is implementation research currently incorporated into each of your goals?
<--- Score

20. Who do we want your customers to become?
<--- Score

21. If you got fired and a new hire took your place, what would she do different?
<--- Score

22. What is your competitive advantage?
<--- Score

23. Do you have the management structure and skills to take on this work?

<--- Score

24. How do you foster innovation?
<--- Score

25. What would have to be true for the option on the table to be the best possible choice?
<--- Score

26. If you were responsible for initiating and implementing major changes in your organization, what steps might you take to ensure acceptance of those changes?
<--- Score

27. What would you recommend your friend do if he/she were facing this dilemma?
<--- Score

28. How do you cross-sell and up-sell your Vendor bid analysis success?
<--- Score

29. What is the recommended frequency of auditing?
<--- Score

30. At what moment would you think; Will I get fired?
<--- Score

31. How do you deal with Vendor bid analysis changes?
<--- Score

32. How do you foster the skills, knowledge, talents, attributes, and characteristics you want to have?
<--- Score

33. How do you transition from the baseline to the target?
<--- Score

34. What is the big Vendor bid analysis idea?
<--- Score

35. Who are your customers?
<--- Score

36. What are the long-term Vendor bid analysis goals?
<--- Score

37. What one word do you want to own in the minds of your customers, employees, and partners?
<--- Score

38. What knowledge, skills and characteristics mark a good Vendor bid analysis project manager?
<--- Score

39. What are you trying to prove to yourself, and how might it be hijacking your life and business success?
<--- Score

40. Are all key stakeholders present at all Structured Walkthroughs?
<--- Score

41. How do you make it meaningful in connecting Vendor bid analysis with what users do day-to-day?
<--- Score

42. How much contingency will be available in the budget?

<--- Score

43. Will it be accepted by users?
<--- Score

44. How likely is it that a customer would recommend your company to a friend or colleague?
<--- Score

45. In retrospect, of the projects that you pulled the plug on, what percent do you wish had been allowed to keep going, and what percent do you wish had ended earlier?
<--- Score

46. What is the estimated value of the project?
<--- Score

47. What Vendor bid analysis skills are most important?
<--- Score

48. Do you have an implicit bias for capital investments over people investments?
<--- Score

49. Who is responsible for ensuring appropriate resources (time, people and money) are allocated to Vendor bid analysis?
<--- Score

50. Can the schedule be done in the given time?
<--- Score

51. What are the short and long-term Vendor bid analysis goals?

<--- Score

52. If you weren't already in this business, would you enter it today? And if not, what are you going to do about it?
<--- Score

53. How does Vendor bid analysis integrate with other stakeholder initiatives?
<--- Score

54. What are strategies for increasing support and reducing opposition?
<--- Score

55. How do you assess the Vendor bid analysis pitfalls that are inherent in implementing it?
<--- Score

56. Which individuals, teams or departments will be involved in Vendor bid analysis?
<--- Score

57. Marketing budgets are tighter, consumers are more skeptical, and social media has changed forever the way we talk about Vendor bid analysis, how do you gain traction?
<--- Score

58. Who will be responsible for deciding whether Vendor bid analysis goes ahead or not after the initial investigations?
<--- Score

59. What projects are going on in the organization today, and what resources are those projects using

from the resource pools?
<--- Score

60. What are the usability implications of Vendor bid analysis actions?
<--- Score

61. Who, on the executive team or the board, has spoken to a customer recently?
<--- Score

62. Has implementation been effective in reaching specified objectives so far?
<--- Score

63. What new services of functionality will be implemented next with Vendor bid analysis ?
<--- Score

64. Who else should you help?
<--- Score

65. Who will manage the integration of tools?
<--- Score

66. How will you insure seamless interoperability of Vendor bid analysis moving forward?
<--- Score

67. Which Vendor bid analysis goals are the most important?
<--- Score

68. Do you know who is a friend or a foe?
<--- Score

69. What threat is Vendor bid analysis addressing?
<--- Score

70. What is your formula for success in Vendor bid analysis ?
<--- Score

71. What are internal and external Vendor bid analysis relations?
<--- Score

72. What are specific Vendor bid analysis rules to follow?
<--- Score

73. What are the challenges?
<--- Score

74. Why should people listen to you?
<--- Score

75. What are you challenging?
<--- Score

76. What do we do when new problems arise?
<--- Score

77. What is the purpose of Vendor bid analysis in relation to the mission?
<--- Score

78. If your company went out of business tomorrow, would anyone who doesn't get a paycheck here care?
<--- Score

79. Are you relevant? Will you be relevant five years

from now? Ten?
<--- Score

80. Have benefits been optimized with all key stakeholders?
<--- Score

81. Who is on the team?
<--- Score

82. Are you maintaining a past–present–future perspective throughout the Vendor bid analysis discussion?
<--- Score

83. Who will provide the final approval of Vendor bid analysis deliverables?
<--- Score

84. Who is responsible for Vendor bid analysis?
<--- Score

85. Why should you adopt a Vendor bid analysis framework?
<--- Score

86. What are current Vendor bid analysis paradigms?
<--- Score

87. How do you create buy-in?
<--- Score

88. How do you accomplish your long range Vendor bid analysis goals?
<--- Score

89. Is maximizing Vendor bid analysis protection the same as minimizing Vendor bid analysis loss?
<--- Score

90. Is a Vendor bid analysis breakthrough on the horizon?
<--- Score

91. What did you miss in the interview for the worst hire you ever made?
<--- Score

92. What is the craziest thing you can do?
<--- Score

93. What is the source of the strategies for Vendor bid analysis strengthening and reform?
<--- Score

94. Would you rather sell to knowledgeable and informed customers or to uninformed customers?
<--- Score

95. How do you keep records, of what?
<--- Score

96. Do you have enough freaky customers in your portfolio pushing you to the limit day in and day out?
<--- Score

97. In the past year, what have you done (or could you have done) to increase the accurate perception of your company/brand as ethical and honest?
<--- Score

98. When information truly is ubiquitous, when

reach and connectivity are completely global, when computing resources are infinite, and when a whole new set of impossibilities are not only possible, but happening, what will that do to your business?
<--- Score

99. Are you / should you be revolutionary or evolutionary?
<--- Score

100. How are you doing compared to your industry?
<--- Score

101. Who have you, as a company, historically been when you've been at your best?
<--- Score

102. What happens when a new employee joins the organization?
<--- Score

103. Political -is anyone trying to undermine this project?
<--- Score

104. What happens if you do not have enough funding?
<--- Score

105. Is it economical; do you have the time and money?
<--- Score

106. Which functions and people interact with the supplier and or customer?
<--- Score

107. Why not do Vendor bid analysis?

<--- Score

108. How do you lead with Vendor bid analysis in mind?

<--- Score

109. Is Vendor bid analysis realistic, or are you setting yourself up for failure?

<--- Score

110. Why is Vendor bid analysis important for you now?

<--- Score

111. What is effective Vendor bid analysis?

<--- Score

112. Is there any existing Vendor bid analysis governance structure?

<--- Score

113. Why is it important to have senior management support for a Vendor bid analysis project?

<--- Score

114. Is Vendor bid analysis dependent on the successful delivery of a current project?

<--- Score

115. Is the impact that Vendor bid analysis has shown?

<--- Score

116. What trouble can you get into?

<--- Score

117. How do you stay inspired?
<--- Score

118. Are you paying enough attention to the partners your company depends on to succeed?
<--- Score

119. Who will determine interim and final deadlines?
<--- Score

120. Do Vendor bid analysis rules make a reasonable demand on a users capabilities?
<--- Score

121. How much does Vendor bid analysis help?
<--- Score

122. What management system can you use to leverage the Vendor bid analysis experience, ideas, and concerns of the people closest to the work to be done?
<--- Score

123. What have you done to protect your business from competitive encroachment?
<--- Score

124. Are you changing as fast as the world around you?
<--- Score

125. Who are four people whose careers you have enhanced?
<--- Score

126. Is your strategy driving your strategy? Or is the way in which you allocate resources driving your strategy?
<--- Score

127. Who is responsible for errors?
<--- Score

128. What role does communication play in the success or failure of a Vendor bid analysis project?
<--- Score

129. What does your signature ensure?
<--- Score

130. What counts that you are not counting?
<--- Score

131. Who uses your product in ways you never expected?
<--- Score

132. Where can you break convention?
<--- Score

133. What is it like to work for you?
<--- Score

134. Are there any activities that you can take off your to do list?
<--- Score

135. What may be the consequences for the performance of an organization if all stakeholders are not consulted regarding Vendor bid analysis?
<--- Score

136. What is a feasible sequencing of reform initiatives over time?
<--- Score

137. What are the gaps in your knowledge and experience?
<--- Score

138. Can you break it down?
<--- Score

139. How do you know if you are successful?
<--- Score

140. How do you keep the momentum going?
<--- Score

141. Ask yourself: how would you do this work if you only had one staff member to do it?
<--- Score

142. How can you incorporate support to ensure safe and effective use of Vendor bid analysis into the services that you provide?
<--- Score

143. What Vendor bid analysis modifications can you make work for you?
<--- Score

144. What should you stop doing?
<--- Score

145. What stupid rule would you most like to kill?
<--- Score

146. What potential megatrends could make your business model obsolete?
<--- Score

147. Operational - will it work?
<--- Score

148. If you find that you havent accomplished one of the goals for one of the steps of the Vendor bid analysis strategy, what will you do to fix it?
<--- Score

149. Do you feel that more should be done in the Vendor bid analysis area?
<--- Score

150. Do you think you know, or do you know you know ?
<--- Score

151. How do you go about securing Vendor bid analysis?
<--- Score

152. What is the kind of project structure that would be appropriate for your Vendor bid analysis project, should it be formal and complex, or can it be less formal and relatively simple?
<--- Score

153. Are your responses positive or negative?
<--- Score

154. Whom among your colleagues do you trust, and for what?

<--- Score

155. If you had to rebuild your organization without any traditional competitive advantages (i.e., no killer technology, promising research, innovative product/ service delivery model, etcetera), how would your people have to approach their work and collaborate together in order to create the necessary conditions for success?
<--- Score

156. Is there a software license agreement that must be signed?
<--- Score

157. Why do and why don't your customers like your organization?
<--- Score

158. Are assumptions made in Vendor bid analysis stated explicitly?
<--- Score

159. Who do you want your customers to become?
<--- Score

160. How will you motivate the stakeholders with the least vested interest?
<--- Score

161. What are the business goals Vendor bid analysis is aiming to achieve?
<--- Score

162. What was the last experiment you ran?
<--- Score

163. Think of your Vendor bid analysis project, what are the main functions?
<--- Score

164. What are your personal philosophies regarding Vendor bid analysis and how do they influence your work?
<--- Score

165. What you are going to do to affect the numbers?
<--- Score

166. Is there a work around that you can use?
<--- Score

167. Is your basic point _____ or _____?
<--- Score

168. Do you see more potential in people than they do in themselves?
<--- Score

169. Can you do all this work?
<--- Score

170. How do you set Vendor bid analysis stretch targets and how do you get people to not only participate in setting these stretch targets but also that they strive to achieve these?
<--- Score

171. Is a Vendor bid analysis team work effort in place?
<--- Score

172. Have new benefits been realized?

<--- Score

173. Do you have the right capabilities and capacities?
<--- Score

174. What will be the consequences to the stakeholder (financial, reputation etc) if Vendor bid analysis does not go ahead or fails to deliver the objectives?
<--- Score

175. If you had to leave your organization for a year and the only communication you could have with employees/colleagues was a single paragraph, what would you write?
<--- Score

176. What business benefits will Vendor bid analysis goals deliver if achieved?
<--- Score

177. Instead of going to current contacts for new ideas, what if you reconnected with dormant contacts--the people you used to know? If you were going reactivate a dormant tie, who would it be?
<--- Score

178. What are your most important goals for the strategic Vendor bid analysis objectives?
<--- Score

179. How can you negotiate Vendor bid analysis successfully with a stubborn boss, an irate client, or a deceitful coworker?
<--- Score

180. Do you say no to customers for no reason?
<--- Score

181. What information is critical to your organization that your executives are ignoring?
<--- Score

182. What is the overall business strategy?
<--- Score

183. What are the potential basics of Vendor bid analysis fraud?
<--- Score

184. What goals did you miss?
<--- Score

185. What is an unauthorized commitment?
<--- Score

186. What must you excel at?
<--- Score

187. Is there any reason to believe the opposite of my current belief?
<--- Score

188. What is the overall talent health of your organization as a whole at senior levels, and for each organization reporting to a member of the Senior Leadership Team?
<--- Score

189. If there were zero limitations, what would you do differently?
<--- Score

190. Do you know what you are doing? And who do you call if you don't?
<--- Score

191. What are the essentials of internal Vendor bid analysis management?
<--- Score

192. How do senior leaders deploy your organizations vision and values through your leadership system, to the workforce, to key suppliers and partners, and to customers and other stakeholders, as appropriate?
<--- Score

193. To whom do you add value?
<--- Score

194. How will you know that the Vendor bid analysis project has been successful?
<--- Score

195. How important is Vendor bid analysis to the user organizations mission?
<--- Score

196. Do you think Vendor bid analysis accomplishes the goals you expect it to accomplish?
<--- Score

197. What are the barriers to increased Vendor bid analysis production?
<--- Score

198. Why will customers want to buy your organizations products/services?

<--- Score

199. What is the funding source for this project?
<--- Score

200. What are the top 3 things at the forefront of your Vendor bid analysis agendas for the next 3 years?
<--- Score

201. Can you maintain your growth without detracting from the factors that have contributed to your success?
<--- Score

202. How do you determine the key elements that affect Vendor bid analysis workforce satisfaction, how are these elements determined for different workforce groups and segments?
<--- Score

203. If you do not follow, then how to lead?
<--- Score

204. Whose voice (department, ethnic group, women, older workers, etc) might you have missed hearing from in your company, and how might you amplify this voice to create positive momentum for your business?
<--- Score

205. How do you govern and fulfill your societal responsibilities?
<--- Score

206. What products and services are you requesting in an RFP?

<--- Score

207. How do you manage Vendor bid analysis Knowledge Management (KM)?
<--- Score

208. How do you engage the workforce, in addition to satisfying them?
<--- Score

209. How do you track customer value, profitability or financial return, organizational success, and sustainability?
<--- Score

210. If no one would ever find out about your accomplishments, how would you lead differently?
<--- Score

Add up total points for this section:
_ _ _ _ _ = Total points for this section

Divided by: _ _ _ _ _ _ (number of statements answered) = _ _ _ _ _ _
Average score for this section

Transfer your score to the Vendor bid analysis Index at the beginning of the Self-Assessment.

Vendor Bid Analysis and Managing Projects, Criteria for Project Managers:

1.0 Initiating Process Group: Vendor Bid Analysis

1. Realistic - are the desired results expressed in a way that the team will be motivated and believe that the required level of involvement will be obtained?

2. Who is behind the Vendor Bid Analysis project?

3. In which Vendor Bid Analysis project management process group is the detailed Vendor Bid Analysis project budget created?

4. What is the NEXT thing to do?

5. During which stage of Risk planning are risks prioritized based on probability and impact?

6. What areas were overlooked on this Vendor Bid Analysis project?

7. How well did the chosen processes fit the needs of the Vendor Bid Analysis project?

8. How will you do it?

9. What will you do to minimize the impact should a risk event occur?

10. Who is involved in each phase?

11. The Vendor Bid Analysis project you are managing has nine stakeholders. How many channel of communications are there between corresponding stakeholders?

12. What business situation is being addressed?

13. When will the Vendor Bid Analysis project be done?

14. First of all, should any action be taken?

15. Do you know if the Vendor Bid Analysis project requires outside equipment or vendor resources?

16. Are there resources to maintain and support the outcome of the Vendor Bid Analysis project?

17. How will it affect me?

18. Do you understand the communication expectations for this Vendor Bid Analysis project?

19. What were things that you need to improve?

20. Are the changes in your Vendor Bid Analysis project being formally requested, analyzed, and approved by the appropriate decision makers?

1.1 Project Charter: Vendor Bid Analysis

21. How high should you set your goals?

22. What barriers do you predict to your success?

23. When is a charter needed?

24. Who are the stakeholders?

25. What are some examples of a business case?

26. Why is it important?

27. Run it as as a startup?

28. When will this occur?

29. Who will take notes, document decisions?

30. What are you striving to accomplish (measurable goal(s))?

31. What does it need to do?

32. For whom?

33. Dependent Vendor Bid Analysis projects: what Vendor Bid Analysis projects must be underway or completed before this Vendor Bid Analysis project can be successful?

34. Is time of the essence?

35. Why have you chosen the aim you have set forth?

36. When?

37. Is it an improvement over existing products?

38. Why is a Vendor Bid Analysis project Charter used?

39. What goes into your Vendor Bid Analysis project Charter?

40. What are the constraints?

1.2 Stakeholder Register: Vendor Bid Analysis

41. Is your organization ready for change?

42. What opportunities exist to provide communications?

43. Who is managing stakeholder engagement?

44. Who wants to talk about Security?

45. How much influence do they have on the Vendor Bid Analysis project?

46. What is the power of the stakeholder?

47. How should employers make voices heard?

48. How will reports be created?

49. How big is the gap?

50. What are the major Vendor Bid Analysis project milestones requiring communications or providing communications opportunities?

51. What & Why?

1.3 Stakeholder Analysis Matrix: Vendor Bid Analysis

52. What do your organizations stakeholders do better than anyone else?

53. How do rules, behaviors affect stakes?

54. How to involve media?

55. Who is influential in the Vendor Bid Analysis project area (both thematic and geographic areas)?

56. How does the Vendor Bid Analysis project involve consultations or collaboration with other organizations?

57. What obstacles does your organization face?

58. What do people from other organizations see as your strengths?

59. Price, value, quality?

60. Technology development and innovation?

61. Political effects?

62. What is your Advocacy Strategy?

63. What mechanisms are proposed to monitor and measure Vendor Bid Analysis project performance in terms of social development outcomes?

64. Resource providers; who can provide resources to ensure the implementation of the Vendor Bid Analysis project?

65. What is the stakeholders mandate, what is mission?

66. Location and geographical?

67. Experience, knowledge, data?

68. Are there people who ise voices or interests in the issue may not be heard?

69. Who is most dependent on the resources at stake?

70. Who will be affected by the work?

71. Cultural, attitudinal, behavioural?

2.0 Planning Process Group: Vendor Bid Analysis

72. What input will you be required to provide the Vendor Bid Analysis project team?

73. Just how important is your work to the overall success of the Vendor Bid Analysis project?

74. When will the Vendor Bid Analysis project be done?

75. How are the principles of aid effectiveness (ownership, alignment, management for development results and mutual responsibility) being applied in the Vendor Bid Analysis project?

76. Vendor Bid Analysis project assessment; why did you do this Vendor Bid Analysis project?

77. To what extent have public/private national resources and/or counterparts been mobilized to contribute to the programs objective and produce results and impacts?

78. Is your organization showing technical capacity and leadership commitment to keep working with the Vendor Bid Analysis project and to repeat it?

79. Does it make any difference if you are successful?

80. Who are the Vendor Bid Analysis project stakeholders?

81. How will you know you did it?

82. How well defined and documented are the Vendor Bid Analysis project management processes you chose to use?

83. Why do it Vendor Bid Analysis projects fail?

84. If action is called for, what form should it take?

85. How well did the chosen processes fit the needs of the Vendor Bid Analysis project?

86. How can you tell when you are done?

87. How do you integrate Vendor Bid Analysis project Planning with the Iterative/Evolutionary SDLC?

88. How will it affect you?

89. What is the critical path for this Vendor Bid Analysis project, and what is the duration of the critical path?

90. Will the products created live up to the necessary quality?

91. Mitigate. what will you do to minimize the impact should a risk event occur?

2.1 Project Management Plan: Vendor Bid Analysis

92. What does management expect of PMs?

93. What data/reports/tools/etc. do your PMs need?

94. What would you do differently what did not work?

95. Was the peer (technical) review of the cost estimates duly coordinated with the cost estimate center of expertise and addressed in the review documentation and certification?

96. Are comparable cost estimates used for comparing, screening and selecting alternative plans, and has a reasonable cost estimate been developed for the recommended plan?

97. Does the selected plan protect privacy?

98. Is the budget realistic?

99. What data/reports/tools/etc. do program managers need?

100. Why do you manage integration?

101. Does the implementation plan have an appropriate division of responsibilities?

102. What worked well?

103. What did not work so well?

104. Do there need to be organizational changes?

105. Did the planning effort collaborate to develop solutions that integrate expertise, policies, programs, and Vendor Bid Analysis projects across entities?

106. How well are you able to manage your risk?

107. If the Vendor Bid Analysis project management plan is a comprehensive document that guides you in Vendor Bid Analysis project execution and control, then what should it NOT contain?

108. What went wrong?

109. Will you add a schedule and diagram?

110. Are cost risk analysis methods applied to develop contingencies for the estimated total Vendor Bid Analysis project costs?

2.2 Scope Management Plan: Vendor Bid Analysis

111. How much money have you spent?

112. Has allowance been made for vacations, holidays, training (learning time for each team member), staff promotions & staff turnovers?

113. Time estimation – how much time will be needed?

114. Can the Vendor Bid Analysis project team do several activities in parallel?

115. What went right?

116. Which statement about customer expectations is not true?

117. Are internal Vendor Bid Analysis project status meetings held at reasonable intervals?

118. Does the Vendor Bid Analysis project have a Quality Culture?

119. Describe the process for accepting the Vendor Bid Analysis project deliverables. Will the Vendor Bid Analysis project deliverables become accepted in writing?

120. What is the relative power of the Vendor Bid Analysis project manager?

121. Do all stakeholders know how to access this repository and where to find the Vendor Bid Analysis project documentation?

122. Process groups – where do scope management processes fit in?

123. What are the risks that could significantly affect the communication on the Vendor Bid Analysis project?

124. The greatest degree of uncertainty is encountered during which phase of the Vendor Bid Analysis project life cycle?

125. Are target dates established for each milestone deliverable?

126. What if you do not have more detailed information on the report?

127. During what part of the PM process is the Vendor Bid Analysis project scope statement created?

128. Personnel with expertise?

129. Have you identified possible roadblocks?

2.3 Requirements Management Plan: Vendor Bid Analysis

130. How will you develop the schedule of requirements activities?

131. Could inaccurate or incomplete requirements in this Vendor Bid Analysis project create a serious risk for the business?

132. How will you communicate scheduled tasks to other team members?

133. Is the user satisfied?

134. How will the requirements become prioritized?

135. What are you trying to do?

136. How often will the reporting occur?

137. Who will finally present the work or product(s) for acceptance?

138. Will you document changes to requirements?

139. How detailed should the Vendor Bid Analysis project get?

140. How will bidders price evaluations be done, by deliverables, phases, or in a big bang?

141. What information regarding the Vendor Bid

Analysis project requirements will be reported?

142. To see if a requirement statement is sufficiently well-defined, read it from the developers perspective. Mentally add the phrase, call me when youre done to the end of the requirement and see if that makes you nervous. In other words, would you need additional clarification from the author to understand the requirement well enough to design and implement it?

143. Is there formal agreement on who has authority to approve a change in requirements?

144. How knowledgeable is the team in the proposed application area?

145. Did you avoid subjective, flowery or non-specific statements?

146. In case of software development; Should you have a test for each code module?

147. When and how will a requirements baseline be established in this Vendor Bid Analysis project?

148. How will requirements be managed?

149. The wbs is developed as part of a joint planning session. and how do you know that youhave done this right?

2.4 Requirements Documentation: Vendor Bid Analysis

150. Is new technology needed?

151. What can tools do for us?

152. How does the proposed Vendor Bid Analysis project contribute to the overall objectives of your organization?

153. Who is interacting with the system?

154. How much testing do you need to do to prove that your system is safe?

155. How will the proposed Vendor Bid Analysis project help?

156. What happens when requirements are wrong?

157. Are all functions required by the customer included?

158. Do technical resources exist?

159. What are current process problems?

160. What facilities must be supported by the system?

161. How will they be documented / shared?

162. What is your Elevator Speech?

163. Can the requirements be checked?

164. What will be the integration problems?

165. Validity. does the system provide the functions which best support the customers needs?

166. How will requirements be documented and who signs off on them?

167. Does the system provide the functions which best support the customers needs?

168. Is your business case still valid?

2.5 Requirements Traceability Matrix: Vendor Bid Analysis

169. What percentage of Vendor Bid Analysis projects are producing traceability matrices between requirements and other work products?

170. How do you manage scope?

171. Is there a requirements traceability process in place?

172. Why do you manage scope?

173. Do you have a clear understanding of all subcontracts in place?

174. What is the WBS?

175. Describe the process for approving requirements so they can be added to the traceability matrix and Vendor Bid Analysis project work can be performed. Will the Vendor Bid Analysis project requirements become approved in writing?

176. Why use a WBS?

177. What are the chronologies, contingencies, consequences, criteria?

178. How will it affect the stakeholders personally in career?

179. How small is small enough?

180. Will you use a Requirements Traceability Matrix?

2.6 Project Scope Statement: Vendor Bid Analysis

181. Which risks does the Vendor Bid Analysis project focus on?

182. What are the possible consequences should a risk come to occur?

183. Elements that deal with providing the detail?

184. Is the scope of your Vendor Bid Analysis project well defined?

185. Is there a baseline plan against which to measure progress?

186. Are the input requirements from the team members clearly documented and communicated?

187. Is the change control process documented and on file?

188. Will the qa related information be reported regularly as part of the status reporting mechanisms?

189. Are there issues that could affect the existing requirements for the result, service, or product if the scope changes?

190. What are the defined meeting materials?

191. Will this process be communicated to the

customer and Vendor Bid Analysis project team?

192. Any new risks introduced or old risks impacted. Are there issues that could affect the existing requirements for the result, service, or product if the scope changes?

193. Why do you need to manage scope?

194. If you were to write a list of what should not be included in the scope statement, what are the things that you would recommend be described as out-of-scope?

195. Is your organization structure appropriate for the Vendor Bid Analysis projects size and complexity?

196. Were key Vendor Bid Analysis project stakeholders brought into the Vendor Bid Analysis project Plan?

197. What are the major deliverables of the Vendor Bid Analysis project?

198. Did your Vendor Bid Analysis project ask for this?

199. Once its defined, what is the stability of the Vendor Bid Analysis project scope?

2.7 Assumption and Constraint Log: Vendor Bid Analysis

200. Security analysis has access to information that is sanitized?

201. Is this model reasonable?

202. Are there processes in place to ensure internal consistency between the source code components?

203. Contradictory information between document sections?

204. Contradictory information between different documents?

205. Does the traceability documentation describe the tool and/or mechanism to be used to capture traceability throughout the life cycle?

206. What strengths do you have?

207. Do you know what your customers expectations are regarding this process?

208. How can constraints be violated?

209. What if failure during recovery?

210. Would known impacts serve as impediments?

211. Should factors be unpredictable over time?

212. Has a Vendor Bid Analysis project Communications Plan been developed?

213. Is the current scope of the Vendor Bid Analysis project substantially different than that originally defined in the approved Vendor Bid Analysis project plan?

214. Have the scope, objectives, costs, benefits and impacts been communicated to all involved and/or impacted stakeholders and work groups?

215. Do the requirements meet the standards of correctness, completeness, consistency, accuracy, and readability?

216. If appropriate, is the deliverable content consistent with current Vendor Bid Analysis project documents and in compliance with the Document Management Plan?

217. How relevant is this attribute to this Vendor Bid Analysis project or audit?

218. What do you log?

2.8 Work Breakdown Structure: Vendor Bid Analysis

219. Do you need another level?

220. Is it a change in scope?

221. How will you and your Vendor Bid Analysis project team define the Vendor Bid Analysis projects scope and work breakdown structure?

222. When does it have to be done?

223. Where does it take place?

224. How much detail?

225. How big is a work-package?

226. Can you make it?

227. Why would you develop a Work Breakdown Structure?

228. Is the work breakdown structure (wbs) defined and is the scope of the Vendor Bid Analysis project clear with assigned deliverable owners?

229. Who has to do it?

230. Is it still viable?

231. How many levels?

232. What is the probability that the Vendor Bid Analysis project duration will exceed xx weeks?

233. What has to be done?

234. How far down?

235. When do you stop?

2.9 WBS Dictionary: Vendor Bid Analysis

236. Is undistributed budget limited to contract effort which cannot yet be planned to CWBS elements at or below the level specified for reporting to the Government?

237. Knowledgeable Vendor Bid Analysis projections of future performance?

238. Are your organizations and items of cost assigned to each pool identified?

239. Changes in the direct base to which overhead costs are allocated?

240. Are overhead cost budgets (or Vendor Bid Analysis projections) established on a facility-wide basis at least annually for the life of the contract?

241. Are meaningful indicators identified for use in measuring the status of cost and schedule performance?

242. Are internal budgets for authorized, and not priced changes based on the contractors resource plan for accomplishing the work?

243. Detailed schedules which support control account and work package start and completion dates/events?

244. Are estimates developed by Vendor Bid Analysis project personnel coordinated with the already stated responsible for overall management to determine whether required resources will be available according to revised planning?

245. Is cost and schedule performance measurement done in a consistent, systematic manner?

246. Does the contractors system description or procedures require that the performance measurement baseline plus management reserve equal the contract budget base?

247. Cwbs elements to be subcontracted, with identification of subcontractors?

248. Can the contractor substantiate work package and planning package budgets?

249. Are indirect costs accumulated for comparison with the corresponding budgets?

250. Are material costs reported within the same period as that in which BCWP is earned for that material?

251. Is all contract work included in the CWBS?

252. Is authorization of budgets in excess of the contract budget base controlled formally and done with the full knowledge and recognition of the procuring activity?

253. What should you drop in order to add something new?

2.10 Schedule Management Plan: Vendor Bid Analysis

254. Can additional resources be added to subsequent tasks to reduce the durations of the already stated tasks?

255. Are cause and effect determined for risks when they occur?

256. Timeline and milestones?

257. Are decisions captured in a decisions log?

258. Does the detailed work plan match the complexity of tasks with the capabilities of personnel?

259. Are the predecessor and successor relationships accurate?

260. Is the schedule vertically and horizontally traceable?

261. Does the resource management plan include a personnel development plan?

262. Are internal Vendor Bid Analysis project status meetings held at reasonable intervals?

263. Is pert / critical path or equivalent methodology being used?

264. Are action items captured and managed?

265. Are the processes for schedule assessment and analysis defined?

266. Is funded schedule margin reasonable and logically distributed?

267. Will the tools selected accomplish the scheduling needs?

268. Time for overtime?

269. Was your organizations estimating methodology being used and followed?

270. Has the ims been resource-loaded and are assigned resources reasonable and available?

271. Are the results of quality assurance reviews provided to affected groups & individuals?

272. Have the key functions and capabilities been defined and assigned to each release or iteration?

273. Do Vendor Bid Analysis project teams & team members report on status / activities / progress?

2.11 Activity List: Vendor Bid Analysis

274. For other activities, how much delay can be tolerated?

275. Who will perform the work?

276. Is infrastructure setup part of your Vendor Bid Analysis project?

277. Where will it be performed?

278. Are the required resources available or need to be acquired?

279. How difficult will it be to do specific activities on this Vendor Bid Analysis project?

280. What is the probability the Vendor Bid Analysis project can be completed in xx weeks?

281. In what sequence?

282. What is the LF and LS for each activity?

283. How should ongoing costs be monitored to try to keep the Vendor Bid Analysis project within budget?

284. When do the individual activities need to start and finish?

285. What are the critical bottleneck activities?

286. What will be performed?

287. What did not go as well?

288. What are you counting on?

289. Should you include sub-activities?

290. How much slack is available in the Vendor Bid Analysis project?

2.12 Activity Attributes: Vendor Bid Analysis

291. Which method produces the more accurate cost assignment?

292. Have you identified the Activity Leveling Priority code value on each activity?

293. Is there a trend during the year?

294. Do you feel very comfortable with your prediction?

295. Can more resources be added?

296. How many resources do you need to complete the work scope within a limit of X number of days?

297. Activity: what is In the Bag?

298. What is missing?

299. Were there other ways you could have organized the data to achieve similar results?

300. Resource is assigned to?

301. Activity: what is Missing?

302. What is your organizations history in doing similar activities?

303. How difficult will it be to do specific activities on this Vendor Bid Analysis project?

304. What is the general pattern here?

305. How much activity detail is required?

306. How many days do you need to complete the work scope with a limit of X number of resources?

307. Can you re-assign any activities to another resource to resolve an over-allocation?

308. How difficult will it be to complete specific activities on this Vendor Bid Analysis project?

2.13 Milestone List: Vendor Bid Analysis

309. Reliability of data, plan predictability?

310. Identify critical paths (one or more) and which activities are on the critical path?

311. What date will the task finish?

312. Do you foresee any technical risks or developmental challenges?

313. What specific improvements did you make to the Vendor Bid Analysis project proposal since the previous time?

314. Who will manage the Vendor Bid Analysis project on a day-to-day basis?

315. Legislative effects?

316. Can you derive how soon can the whole Vendor Bid Analysis project finish?

317. Calculate how long can activity be delayed?

318. Describe the concept of the technology, product or service that will be or has been developed. How will it be used?

319. Effects on core activities, distraction?

320. Loss of key staff?

321. How late can each activity be finished and started?

322. Continuity, supply chain robustness?

323. Global influences?

324. How soon can the activity start?

325. What would happen if a delivery of material was one week late?

326. How late can the activity finish?

327. How do you manage time?

2.14 Network Diagram: Vendor Bid Analysis

328. If a current contract exists, can you provide the vendor name, contract start, and contract expiration date?

329. If the Vendor Bid Analysis project network diagram cannot change and you have extra personnel resources, what is the BEST thing to do?

330. Are you on time?

331. How confident can you be in your milestone dates and the delivery date?

332. What activities must occur simultaneously with this activity?

333. Planning: who, how long, what to do?

334. Which type of network diagram allows you to depict four types of dependencies?

335. What controls the start and finish of a job?

336. Can you calculate the confidence level?

337. Review the logical flow of the network diagram. Take a look at which activities you have first and then sequence the activities. Do they make sense?

338. If x is long, what would be the completion time

if you break x into two parallel parts of y weeks and z weeks?

339. What job or jobs precede it?

340. What are the Major Administrative Issues?

341. What job or jobs could run concurrently?

342. What must be completed before an activity can be started?

343. Are the required resources available?

344. What are the tools?

345. Why must you schedule milestones, such as reviews, throughout the Vendor Bid Analysis project?

2.15 Activity Resource Requirements: Vendor Bid Analysis

346. Why do you do that?

347. How many signatures do you require on a check and does this match what is in your policy and procedures?

348. What is the Work Plan Standard?

349. Organizational Applicability?

350. What are constraints that you might find during the Human Resource Planning process?

351. Anything else?

352. Other support in specific areas?

353. When does monitoring begin?

354. Do you use tools like decomposition and rolling-wave planning to produce the activity list and other outputs?

355. Which logical relationship does the PDM use most often?

356. Are there unresolved issues that need to be addressed?

357. Is there anything planned that does not need to

be here?

358. How do you handle petty cash?

2.16 Resource Breakdown Structure: Vendor Bid Analysis

359. What defines a successful Vendor Bid Analysis project?

360. Who needs what information?

361. What is the primary purpose of the human resource plan?

362. What defines a successful Vendor Bid Analysis project?

363. Why is this important?

364. How difficult will it be to do specific activities on this Vendor Bid Analysis project?

365. What is Vendor Bid Analysis project communication management?

366. What is the purpose of assigning and documenting responsibility?

367. What can you do to improve productivity?

368. Which resource planning tool provides information on resource responsibility and accountability?

369. Who will use the system?

370. What is the number one predictor of a groups productivity?

371. Is predictive resource analysis being done?

372. Who is allowed to see what data about which resources?

373. Who will be used as a Vendor Bid Analysis project team member?

374. Who delivers the information?

2.17 Activity Duration Estimates: Vendor Bid Analysis

375. Do checklists exist that list frequently performed activities?

376. Are measurement techniques employed to determine the potential impact of proposed changes?

377. What type of information goes in a quality assurance plan?

378. Are adjustments implemented to correct or prevent defects?

379. Does a process exist to identify which qualified resources may be attainable?

380. On which process should team members spend the most time?

381. Calculate the expected duration for an activity that has a most likely time of 5, a pessimistic time of 13, and a optimiztic time of 3?

382. Will it help promote wellness at your organization and reduce insurance costs?

383. Does a process exist to formally recognize new Vendor Bid Analysis projects?

384. Will the new application be developed using existing hardware, software, and networks?

385. Vendor Bid Analysis project manager has received activity duration estimates from his team. Which does one need in order to complete schedule development?

386. Are reward and recognition systems defined to promote or reinforce desired behavior?

387. Could it have been avoided?

388. What is the career outlook for Vendor Bid Analysis project managers in information technology?

389. What is pmp certification, and why do you think the number of people earning it has grown so much in the past ten years?

390. What is wrong with this scenario?

391. What are the main parts of a scope statement?

392. Are processes defined to monitor Vendor Bid Analysis project cost and schedule variances?

393. Does a procedure exist to ensure the Vendor Bid Analysis project work is completed in the appropriate sequence and on time?

394. What does it mean to take a systems view of a Vendor Bid Analysis project?

2.18 Duration Estimating Worksheet: Vendor Bid Analysis

395. When does your organization expect to be able to complete it?

396. What utility impacts are there?

397. How can the Vendor Bid Analysis project be displayed graphically to better visualize the activities?

398. Done before proceeding with this activity or what can be done concurrently?

399. What is next?

400. What work will be included in the Vendor Bid Analysis project?

401. What is an Average Vendor Bid Analysis project?

402. Why estimate time and cost?

403. Is this operation cost effective?

404. Is the Vendor Bid Analysis project responsive to community need?

405. What is your role?

406. What is cost and Vendor Bid Analysis project cost management?

407. How should ongoing costs be monitored to try to keep the Vendor Bid Analysis project within budget?

408. Value pocket identification & quantification what are value pockets?

409. When, then?

410. What questions do you have?

411. What info is needed?

2.19 Project Schedule: Vendor Bid Analysis

412. How do you use schedules?

413. What is the difference?

414. Is there a Schedule Management Plan that establishes the criteria and activities for developing, monitoring and controlling the Vendor Bid Analysis project schedule?

415. Eliminate unnecessary activities. Are there activities that came from a template or previous Vendor Bid Analysis project that are not applicable on this phase of this Vendor Bid Analysis project?

416. How can slack be negative?

417. If there are any qualifying green components to this Vendor Bid Analysis project, what portion of the total Vendor Bid Analysis project cost is green?

418. How can you shorten the schedule?

419. Why do you need schedules?

420. Why is software Vendor Bid Analysis project disaster so common?

421. Are key risk mitigation strategies added to the Vendor Bid Analysis project schedule?

422. Are activities connected because logic dictates the order in which others occur?

423. How can you address that situation?

424. Why time management?

425. Should you have a test for each code module?

426. Change management required?

427. Is the Vendor Bid Analysis project schedule available for all Vendor Bid Analysis project team members to review?

428. Understand the constraints used in preparing the schedule. Are activities connected because logic dictates the order in which others occur?

429. Why is this particularly bad?

430. How do you know that youhave done this right?

431. How can you minimize or control changes to Vendor Bid Analysis project schedules?

2.20 Cost Management Plan: Vendor Bid Analysis

432. Cost management – how will the cost of changes be estimated and controlled?

433. Are risk triggers captured?

434. Has a quality assurance plan been developed for the Vendor Bid Analysis project?

435. Why do you manage cost?

436. Does the business case include how the Vendor Bid Analysis project aligns with your organizations strategic goals & objectives?

437. Are updated Vendor Bid Analysis project time & resource estimates reasonable based on the current Vendor Bid Analysis project stage?

438. What is cost and Vendor Bid Analysis project cost management?

439. Time management – how will the schedule impact of changes be estimated and approved?

440. What is your organizations history in doing similar tasks?

441. Are actuals compared against estimates to analyze and correct variances?

442. Scope of work – What is the likelihood and extent of potential future changes to the Vendor Bid Analysis project scope?

443. Are changes in scope (deliverable commitments) agreed to by all affected groups & individuals?

444. Have the reasons why the changes to your organizational systems and capabilities are required?

445. Are the Vendor Bid Analysis project team members located locally to the users/stakeholders?

446. Are mitigation strategies identified?

447. Are meeting minutes captured and sent out after the meeting?

448. Is it possible to track all classes of Vendor Bid Analysis project work (e.g. scheduled, un-scheduled, defect repair, etc.)?

449. Owner, contractor, and subcontractors?

450. Vendor Bid Analysis project Objectives?

2.21 Activity Cost Estimates: Vendor Bid Analysis

451. Who & what determines the need for contracted services?

452. In which phase of the acquisition process cycle does source qualifications reside?

453. What were things that you did well, and could improve, and how?

454. How do you change activities?

455. What is the Vendor Bid Analysis projects sustainability strategy that will ensure Vendor Bid Analysis project results will endure or be sustained?

456. Does the activity rely on a common set of tools to carry it out?

457. How difficult will it be to do specific tasks on the Vendor Bid Analysis project?

458. How and when do you enter into Vendor Bid Analysis project Procurement Management?

459. One way to define activities is to consider how organization employees describe jobs to families and friends. You basically want to know, What do you do?

460. Who determines the quality and expertise of contractors?

461. Review – what are some common errors in activities to avoid?

462. Was the consultant knowledgeable about the program?

463. Were the tasks or work products prepared by the consultant useful?

464. Were you satisfied with the work?

465. What makes a good expected result statement?

466. How do you fund change orders?

467. Did the consultant work with local staff to develop local capacity?

468. What is a Vendor Bid Analysis project Management Plan?

469. When do you enter into PPM?

470. Is there anything unique in this Vendor Bid Analysis projects scope statement that will affect resources?

2.22 Cost Estimating Worksheet: Vendor Bid Analysis

471. What happens to any remaining funds not used?

472. Ask: are others positioned to know, are others credible, and will others cooperate?

473. What additional Vendor Bid Analysis project(s) could be initiated as a result of this Vendor Bid Analysis project?

474. What is the estimated labor cost today based upon this information?

475. Does the Vendor Bid Analysis project provide innovative ways for stakeholders to overcome obstacles or deliver better outcomes?

476. How will the results be shared and to whom?

477. Is it feasible to establish a control group arrangement?

478. What can be included?

479. Is the Vendor Bid Analysis project responsive to community need?

480. Who is best positioned to know and assist in identifying corresponding factors?

481. Can a trend be established from historical

performance data on the selected measure and are the criteria for using trend analysis or forecasting methods met?

482. What will others want?

483. What costs are to be estimated?

484. Will the Vendor Bid Analysis project collaborate with the local community and leverage resources?

485. What is the purpose of estimating?

486. Identify the timeframe necessary to monitor progress and collect data to determine how the selected measure has changed?

2.23 Cost Baseline: Vendor Bid Analysis

487. What weaknesses do you have?

488. Have you identified skills that are missing from your team?

489. Has the appropriate access to relevant data and analysis capability been granted?

490. Have all approved changes to the schedule baseline been identified and impact on the Vendor Bid Analysis project documented?

491. Escalation criteria met?

492. On budget?

493. How do you manage cost?

494. Has the actual cost of the Vendor Bid Analysis project (or Vendor Bid Analysis project phase) been tallied and compared to the approved budget?

495. Have all approved changes to the cost baseline been identified and impact on the Vendor Bid Analysis project documented?

496. Are you meeting with your team regularly?

497. What is the reality?

498. If you sold 10x widgets on a day, what would the affect on profits be?

499. Vendor Bid Analysis project goals -should others be reconsidered?

500. Does a process exist for establishing a cost baseline to measure Vendor Bid Analysis project performance?

501. Is the cr within Vendor Bid Analysis project scope?

502. Does it impact schedule, cost, quality?

503. Are there contingencies or conditions related to the acceptance?

2.24 Quality Management Plan: Vendor Bid Analysis

504. How do you document and correct nonconformances?

505. How will you know that a change is actually an improvement?

506. How does your organization address regulatory, legal, and ethical compliance?

507. What are the appropriate test methods to be used?

508. You know what your customers expectations are regarding this process?

509. How does your organization make it easy for customers to seek assistance or complain?

510. Does the program use modeling in the permitting or decision-making processes?

511. How is staff trained on the recording of field notes?

512. How relevant is this attribute to this Vendor Bid Analysis project or audit?

513. Show/provide copy of procedures for taking field notes?

514. Have all necessary approvals been obtained?

515. Does the program use other agents to collect samples?

516. What are you trying to accomplish?

517. How do you decide what information needs to be recorded?

518. Are there ways to reduce the time it takes to get something approved?

519. Who is approving the QAPP?

520. Who gets results of work?

521. Are there nonconformance issues?

522. Were there any deficiencies / issues identified in the prior years self-assessment?

2.25 Quality Metrics: Vendor Bid Analysis

523. Who notifies stakeholders of normal and abnormal results?

524. Where did complaints, returns and warranty claims come from?

525. What makes a visualization memorable?

526. Should a modifier be included?

527. What is the timeline to meet your goal?

528. Can you correlate your quality metrics to profitability?

529. How do you calculate such metrics?

530. What percentage are outcome-based?

531. What do you measure?

532. What metrics do you measure?

533. Has risk analysis been adequately reviewed?

534. When will the Final Guidance will be issued?

535. What level of statistical confidence do you use?

536. Was material distributed on time?

537. Where is quality now?

538. How do you measure?

539. What method of measurement do you use?

540. Are applicable standards referenced and available?

2.26 Process Improvement Plan: Vendor Bid Analysis

541. Management commitment at all levels?

542. Modeling current processes is great, and will you ever see a return on that investment?

543. Does your process ensure quality?

544. Where do you want to be?

545. Are you following the quality standards?

546. Everyone agrees on what process improvement is, right?

547. Are there forms and procedures to collect and record the data?

548. The motive is determined by asking, Why do you want to achieve this goal?

549. Why quality management?

550. To elicit goal statements, do you ask a question such as, What do you want to achieve?

551. What makes people good SPI coaches?

552. Where do you focus?

553. What personnel are the change agents for your

initiative?

554. What is the return on investment?

555. How do you manage quality?

556. Are you making progress on the goals?

557. Are you meeting the quality standards?

558. If a process improvement framework is being used, which elements will help the problems and goals listed?

2.27 Responsibility Assignment Matrix: Vendor Bid Analysis

559. How many people do you need?

560. Are all elements of indirect expense identified to overhead cost budgets of Vendor Bid Analysis projections?

561. What materials and procurements needed?

562. Is the entire contract planned in time-phased control accounts to the extent practicable?

563. Authorization to proceed with all authorized work?

564. Is every signing-off responsibility and every communicating responsibility critically necessary?

565. What will the work cost?

566. Are others working on the right things?

567. Are too many reports done in writing instead of verbally?

568. How do you assist them to be as productive as possible?

569. Will too many Communicating responsibilities tangle the Vendor Bid Analysis project in unnecessary communications?

570. What expertise is not available in your department?

571. Does the contractor use objective results, design reviews and tests to trace schedule performance?

572. Budgets assigned to major functional organizations?

573. If a role has only Signing-off, or only Communicating responsibility and has no Performing, Accountable, or Monitoring responsibility, is it necessary?

574. Does a missing responsibility indicate that the current Vendor Bid Analysis project is not yet fully understood?

575. Contemplated overhead expenditure for each period based on the best information currently available?

576. Do you need to convince people that its well worth the time and effort?

2.28 Roles and Responsibilities: Vendor Bid Analysis

577. What areas would you highlight for changes or improvements?

578. Do the values and practices inherent in the culture of your organization foster or hinder the process?

579. To decide whether to use a quality measurement, ask how will you know when it is achieved?

580. Are governance roles and responsibilities documented?

581. What should you highlight for improvement?

582. Does the team have access to and ability to use data analysis tools?

583. What is working well?

584. How is your work-life balance?

585. Who is responsible for implementation activities and where will the functions, roles and responsibilities be defined?

586. What are your major roles and responsibilities in the area of performance measurement and assessment?

587. What should you do now to ensure that you are meeting all expectations of your current position?

588. Required skills, knowledge, experience?

589. Does your vision/mission support a culture of quality data?

590. Influence: what areas of organizational decision making are you able to influence when you do not have authority to make the final decision?

591. Was the expectation clearly communicated?

592. Are your budgets supportive of a culture of quality data?

593. Is the data complete?

594. Accountabilities: what are the roles and responsibilities of individual team members?

595. Concern: where are you limited or have no authority, where you can not influence?

596. Who is involved?

2.29 Human Resource Management Plan: Vendor Bid Analysis

597. How can below standard performers be guided/ developed to upgrade performance?

598. Is the manpower level sufficient to meet the future business requirements?

599. Are all payments made according to the contract(s)?

600. Vendor Bid Analysis project Objectives?

601. Is the Vendor Bid Analysis project sponsor clearly communicating the business case or rationale for why this Vendor Bid Analysis project is needed?

602. Has the scope management document been updated and distributed to help prevent scope creep?

603. Are there dependencies with other initiatives or Vendor Bid Analysis projects?

604. Alignment to strategic goals & objectives?

605. Do all stakeholders know how to access this repository and where to find the Vendor Bid Analysis project documentation?

606. Are the Vendor Bid Analysis project plans updated on a frequent basis?

607. Were Vendor Bid Analysis project team members involved in the development of activity & task decomposition?

608. Has a capability assessment been conducted?

609. Are vendor invoices audited for accuracy before payment?

610. Are meeting objectives identified for each meeting?

611. How complete is the human resource management plan?

612. Does the schedule include Vendor Bid Analysis project management time and change request analysis time?

613. What were things that you did very well and want to do the same again on the next Vendor Bid Analysis project?

614. Is this Vendor Bid Analysis project carried out in partnership with other groups/organizations?

2.30 Communications Management Plan: Vendor Bid Analysis

615. Are the stakeholders getting the information others need, are others consulted, are concerns addressed?

616. Who needs to know and how much?

617. Do you then often overlook a key stakeholder or stakeholder group?

618. How much time does it take to do it?

619. What is the stakeholders level of authority?

620. Who to share with?

621. Are there too many who have an interest in some aspect of your work?

622. How is this initiative related to other portfolios, programs, or Vendor Bid Analysis projects?

623. What approaches do you use?

624. Who did you turn to if you had questions?

625. What to learn?

626. Which team member will work with each stakeholder?

627. Why is stakeholder engagement important?

628. What to know?

629. Why do you manage communications?

630. Where do team members get information?

631. Are others needed?

632. Are there common objectives between the team and the stakeholder?

633. Is there an important stakeholder who is actively opposed and will not receive messages?

2.31 Risk Management Plan: Vendor Bid Analysis

634. Do you manage the process through use of metrics?

635. What are it-specific requirements?

636. What other risks are created by choosing an avoidance strategy?

637. Does the software engineering team have the right mix of skills?

638. Havent software Vendor Bid Analysis projects been late before?

639. Are end-users enthusiastically committed to the Vendor Bid Analysis project and the system/product to be built?

640. Financial risk: can your organization afford to undertake the Vendor Bid Analysis project?

641. Minimize cost and financial risk?

642. Was an original risk assessment/risk management plan completed?

643. Do you have a mechanism for managing change?

644. Are testing tools available and suitable?

645. Workarounds are determined during which step of risk management?

646. Can the risk be avoided by choosing a different alternative?

647. People risk -are people with appropriate skills available to help complete the Vendor Bid Analysis project?

648. Technology risk: is the Vendor Bid Analysis project technically feasible?

649. Which risks should get the attention?

650. Is there additional information that would make you more confident about your analysis?

651. Risk probability and impact: how will the probabilities and impacts of risk items be assessed?

652. Do benefits and chances of success outweigh potential damage if success is not attained?

653. How is implementation of risk actions performed?

2.32 Risk Register: Vendor Bid Analysis

654. Who is accountable?

655. What are the main aims, objectives of the policy, strategy, or service and the intended outcomes?

656. What is the appropriate level of risk management for this Vendor Bid Analysis project?

657. User involvement: do you have the right users?

658. Who needs to know about this?

659. What action, if any, has been taken to respond to the risk?

660. People risk -are people with appropriate skills available to help complete the Vendor Bid Analysis project?

661. Assume the risk event or situation happens, what would the impact be?

662. Why would you develop a risk register?

663. Financial risk -can your organization afford to undertake the Vendor Bid Analysis project?

664. How well are risks controlled?

665. Who is going to do it?

666. How could corresponding Risk affect the Vendor Bid Analysis project in terms of cost and schedule?

667. Are there other alternative controls that could be implemented?

668. Risk documentation: what reporting formats and processes will be used for risk management activities?

669. Is further information required before making a decision?

670. What should you do when?

671. What is a Community Risk Register?

672. How often will the Risk Management Plan and Risk Register be formally reviewed, and by whom?

673. Risk categories: what are the main categories of risks that should be addressed on this Vendor Bid Analysis project?

2.33 Probability and Impact Assessment: Vendor Bid Analysis

674. Can you avoid altogether some things that might go wrong?

675. Are end-users enthusiastically committed to the Vendor Bid Analysis project and the system/product to be built?

676. How carefully have the potential competitors been identified?

677. What are the levels of understanding of the future users of the outcome/results of this Vendor Bid Analysis project?

678. What risks are necessary to achieve success?

679. What is the likely future demand of the customer?

680. What should be the requirement of organizational restructuring as each subVendor Bid Analysis project goes through a different lifecycle phase?

681. Are team members trained in the use of the tools?

682. Does the Vendor Bid Analysis project team have experience with the technology to be implemented?

683. How realistic is the timing of introduction?

684. What things are likely to change?

685. Mitigation -how can you avoid the risk?

686. Are Vendor Bid Analysis project requirements stable?

687. Who will be responsible for a slippage?

688. What significant shift will occur in governmental policies, laws, and regulations pertaining to specific industries?

689. To what extent is the chosen technology maturing?

690. What would be the effect of slippage?

691. Are the facilities, expertise, resources, and management know-how available to handle the situation?

692. How do you define a risk?

693. Can you stabilize dynamic risk factors?

2.34 Probability and Impact Matrix: Vendor Bid Analysis

694. What are the uncertainties associated with the technology selected for the Vendor Bid Analysis project?

695. Have top software and customer managers formally committed to support the Vendor Bid Analysis project?

696. Who should be notified of the occurrence of each of the risk indicators?

697. Is the customer technically sophisticated in the product area?

698. Who are the owners?

699. What are the current or emerging trends of culture?

700. What will the damage be?

701. What should be done with risks on the watch list?

702. What are ways to measure and evaluate risks?

703. How much risk do others need to take?

704. Do you use any methods to analyze risks?

705. How risk averse are you?

706. Amount of reused software?

707. Does the customer have a solid idea of what is required?

708. What should you do FIRST?

709. Non-valid or incredible information?

710. Do you know the order of planning yet?

711. Has the need for the Vendor Bid Analysis project been properly established?

2.35 Risk Data Sheet: Vendor Bid Analysis

712. Who has a vested interest in how you perform as your organization (our stakeholders)?

713. Risk of what?

714. Has a sensitivity analysis been carried out?

715. If it happens, what are the consequences?

716. What is the likelihood of it happening?

717. What do people affected think about the need for, and practicality of preventive measures?

718. What if client refuses?

719. How can hazards be reduced?

720. What was measured?

721. What can you do?

722. What is the environment within which you operate (social trends, economic, community values, broad based participation, national directions etc.)?

723. What can happen?

724. Has the most cost-effective solution been chosen?

725. What are the main opportunities available to you that you should grab while you can?

726. How reliable is the data source?

727. Will revised controls lead to tolerable risk levels?

728. Whom do you serve (customers)?

729. What are the main threats to your existence?

730. What will be the consequences if the risk happens?

2.36 Procurement Management Plan: Vendor Bid Analysis

731. Is the structure for tracking the Vendor Bid Analysis project schedule well defined and assigned to a specific individual?

732. How long will it take for the purchase cost to be the same as the lease cost?

733. Is there an onboarding process in place?

734. Is there a Steering Committee in place?

735. Do all stakeholders know how to access the PM repository and where to find the Vendor Bid Analysis project documentation?

736. Are all key components of a Quality Assurance Plan present?

737. Is it standard practice to formally commit stakeholders to the Vendor Bid Analysis project via agreements?

738. Are all resource assumptions documented?

739. Have Vendor Bid Analysis project team accountabilities & responsibilities been clearly defined?

740. Is the Vendor Bid Analysis project sponsor clearly communicating the business case or rationale for why

this Vendor Bid Analysis project is needed?

741. Is the assigned Vendor Bid Analysis project manager a PMP (Certified Vendor Bid Analysis project manager) and experienced?

742. Has the business need been clearly defined?

743. What are your quality assurance overheads?

744. Have external dependencies been captured in the schedule?

745. Are staff skills known and available for each task?

746. Is there a Quality Management Plan?

747. Vendor Bid Analysis project Objectives?

748. Financial capacity; does the seller have, or can the seller reasonably be expected to obtain, the financial resources needed?

749. Has Vendor Bid Analysis project success criteria been defined?

2.37 Source Selection Criteria: Vendor Bid Analysis

750. What is the effect of the debriefing schedule on potential protests?

751. When is it appropriate to issue a Draft Request for Proposal (DRFP)?

752. What should a Draft Request for Proposal (DRFP) include?

753. How do you encourage efficiency and consistency?

754. How do you ensure an integrated assessment of proposals?

755. What are the steps in performing a cost/tech tradeoff?

756. When must you conduct a debriefing?

757. Is there collaboration among your evaluators?

758. What are the guiding principles for developing an evaluation report?

759. How are clarifications and communications appropriately used?

760. What should be considered?

761. With the rapid changes in information technology, will media be readable in five or ten years?

762. How and when do you enter into Vendor Bid Analysis project Procurement Management?

763. Which contract type places the most risk on the seller?

764. What information may not be provided?

765. Is experience evaluated?

766. Do you have a plan to document consensus results including disposition of any disagreement by individual evaluators?

767. What management structure does your organization consider as optimal for performing the contract?

768. Can you make a cost/technical tradeoff?

769. Do you prepare an independent cost estimate?

2.38 Stakeholder Management Plan: Vendor Bid Analysis

770. Were Vendor Bid Analysis project team members involved in the development of activity & task decomposition?

771. What would you gain if you spent time working to improve this process?

772. How many Vendor Bid Analysis project staff does this specific process affect?

773. What is the primary function of the Activity Decomposition Decision Tree?

774. Are estimating assumptions and constraints captured?

775. Is there a set of procedures defining the scope, procedures, and deliverables defining quality control?

776. What information should be collected?

777. Are there any potential occupational health and safety issues due to the proposed purchases?

778. Are all vendor contracts closed out?

779. Are assumptions being identified, recorded, analyzed, qualified and closed?

780. Is there a formal set of procedures supporting

Stakeholder Management?

781. How accurate and complete is the information?

782. Is the communication plan being followed?

783. Which risks pose the highest threat?

784. Are multiple estimation methods being employed?

785. Is a pmo (Vendor Bid Analysis project management office) in place and does it provide oversight to the Vendor Bid Analysis project?

786. Is there an issues management plan in place?

2.39 Change Management Plan: Vendor Bid Analysis

787. How many people are required in each of the roles?

788. What type of materials/channels will be available to leverage?

789. Identify the risk and assess the significance and likelihood of it occurring and plan the contingency What risks may occur upfront?

790. What tasks are needed?

791. Has this been negotiated with the customer and sponsor?

792. Is there a need for new relationships to be built?

793. When does it make sense to customize?

794. What policies and procedures need to be changed?

795. Would you need to tailor a special message for each segment of the audience?

796. Have the systems been configured and tested?

797. How will the stakeholders share information and transfer knowledge?

798. What do you expect the target audience to do, say, think or feel as a result of this communication?

799. Who in the business it includes?

800. Has the training co-ordinator been provided with the training details and put in place the necessary arrangements?

801. Will you need new processes?

802. Where will the funds come from?

803. How does the principle of senders and receivers make the Vendor Bid Analysis project communications effort more complex?

804. When should a given message be communicated?

805. Are there resource implications for your communications strategy?

3.0 Executing Process Group: Vendor Bid Analysis

806. Would you rate yourself as being risk-averse, risk-neutral, or risk-seeking?

807. What are deliverables of your Vendor Bid Analysis project?

808. How could stakeholders negatively impact your Vendor Bid Analysis project?

809. Who are the Vendor Bid Analysis project stakeholders?

810. Will a new application be developed using existing hardware, software, and networks?

811. Do schedule issues conflicts?

812. What is the difference between using brainstorming and the Delphi technique for risk identification?

813. What are the challenges Vendor Bid Analysis project teams face?

814. What are some crucial elements of a good Vendor Bid Analysis project plan?

815. Does software appear easy to learn?

816. Will outside resources be needed to help?

817. How well did the team follow the chosen processes?

818. What are the main processes included in Vendor Bid Analysis project quality management?

819. How many different communication channels does the Vendor Bid Analysis project team have?

820. Based on your Vendor Bid Analysis project communication management plan, what worked well?

821. Does the case present a realistic scenario?

822. What areas were overlooked on this Vendor Bid Analysis project?

823. How does a Vendor Bid Analysis project life cycle differ from a product life cycle?

824. What is in place for ensuring adequate change control on Vendor Bid Analysis projects that involve outside contracts?

825. What communication items need improvement?

3.1 Team Member Status Report: Vendor Bid Analysis

826. Are your organizations Vendor Bid Analysis projects more successful over time?

827. How much risk is involved?

828. What specific interest groups do you have in place?

829. Why is it to be done?

830. The problem with Reward & Recognition Programs is that the truly deserving people all too often get left out. How can you make it practical?

831. Does every department have to have a Vendor Bid Analysis project Manager on staff?

832. Are the attitudes of staff regarding Vendor Bid Analysis project work improving?

833. What is to be done?

834. How will resource planning be done?

835. When a teams productivity and success depend on collaboration and the efficient flow of information, what generally fails them?

836. Are the products of your organizations Vendor Bid Analysis projects meeting customers objectives?

837. Do you have an Enterprise Vendor Bid Analysis project Management Office (EPMO)?

838. Will the staff do training or is that done by a third party?

839. How it is to be done?

840. Does your organization have the means (staff, money, contract, etc.) to produce or to acquire the product, good, or service?

841. Does the product, good, or service already exist within your organization?

842. How can you make it practical?

843. How does this product, good, or service meet the needs of the Vendor Bid Analysis project and your organization as a whole?

844. Is there evidence that staff is taking a more professional approach toward management of your organizations Vendor Bid Analysis projects?

3.2 Change Request: Vendor Bid Analysis

845. What are the basic mechanics of the Change Advisory Board (CAB)?

846. Does the schedule include Vendor Bid Analysis project management time and change request analysis time?

847. Change request coordination ?

848. Who is responsible for the implementation and monitoring of all measures?

849. Will all change requests be unconditionally tracked through this process?

850. How do team members communicate with each other?

851. Who will perform the change?

852. Has your address changed?

853. Screen shots or attachments included in a Change Request?

854. Will there be a change request form in use?

855. What is the relationship between requirements attributes and attributes like complexity and size?

856. Who is communicating the change?

857. When do you create a change request?

858. How is the change documented (format, content, storage)?

859. Who has responsibility for approving and ranking changes?

860. What are the duties of the change control team?

861. Is it feasible to use requirements attributes as predictors of reliability?

862. How does a team identify the discrete elements of a configuration?

863. How many times must the change be modified or presented to the change control board before it is approved?

864. Will the change use memory to the extent that other functions will be not have sufficient memory to operate effectively?

3.3 Change Log: Vendor Bid Analysis

865. Should a more thorough impact analysis be conducted?

866. Is this a mandatory replacement?

867. Who initiated the change request?

868. When was the request approved?

869. Is the change request within Vendor Bid Analysis project scope?

870. How does this change affect the timeline of the schedule?

871. Will the Vendor Bid Analysis project fail if the change request is not executed?

872. Is the submitted change a new change or a modification of a previously approved change?

873. Do the described changes impact on the integrity or security of the system?

874. Is the requested change request a result of changes in other Vendor Bid Analysis project(s)?

875. How does this change affect scope?

876. When was the request submitted?

877. Is the change backward compatible without

limitations?

878. Is the change request open, closed or pending?

879. Does the suggested change request seem to represent a necessary enhancement to the product?

880. Where do changes come from?

881. Does the suggested change request represent a desired enhancement to the products functionality?

882. How does this relate to the standards developed for specific business processes?

3.4 Decision Log: Vendor Bid Analysis

883. How does an increasing emphasis on cost containment influence the strategies and tactics used?

884. What makes you different or better than others companies selling the same thing?

885. How do you define success?

886. What is your overall strategy for quality control / quality assurance procedures?

887. Is your opponent open to a non-traditional workflow, or will it likely challenge anything you do?

888. It becomes critical to track and periodically revisit both operational effectiveness; Are you noticing all that you need to, and are you interpreting what you see effectively?

889. Adversarial environment. is your opponent open to a non-traditional workflow, or will it likely challenge anything you do?

890. How effective is maintaining the log at facilitating organizational learning?

891. Who is the decisionmaker?

892. Is everything working as expected?

893. Meeting purpose; why does this team meet?

894. What is the line where eDiscovery ends and document review begins?

895. Does anything need to be adjusted?

896. What eDiscovery problem or issue did your organization set out to fix or make better?

897. Behaviors; what are guidelines that the team has identified that will assist them with getting the most out of team meetings?

898. At what point in time does loss become unacceptable?

899. Who will be given a copy of this document and where will it be kept?

900. Linked to original objective?

901. Which variables make a critical difference?

902. How do you know when you are achieving it?

3.5 Quality Audit: Vendor Bid Analysis

903. How does your organization know that its general support services planning and management systems are appropriately effective and constructive?

904. How does your organization know that its staff placements are appropriately effective and constructive in relation to program-related learning outcomes?

905. How does your organization know that its Mission, Vision and Values Statements are appropriate and effectively guiding your organization?

906. What are your supplier audits?

907. How does your organization know that its management system is appropriately effective and constructive?

908. What are you trying to accomplish with this audit?

909. How does your organization know that its system for ensuring that its training activities are appropriately resourced and support is appropriately effective and constructive?

910. How does your organization know that its relationships with relevant professional bodies are appropriately effective and constructive?

911. What data about organizational performance is

routinely collected and reported?

912. How does your organization know that its relationships with other relevant organizations are appropriately effective and constructive?

913. How does your organization know that its system for supporting staff research capability is appropriately effective and constructive?

914. Are training programs documented?

915. Does the audit organization have experience in performing the required work for entities of your type and size?

916. How does your organization know whether they are adhering to mission and achieving objectives?

917. How does your organization know that the system for managing its facilities is appropriately effective and constructive?

918. How does your organization know that its staffing profile is optimally aligned with the capability requirements implicit (or explicit) in its Strategic Plan?

919. Are all employees made aware of device defects which may occur from the improper performance of specific jobs?

920. How does your organization know that its research programs are appropriately effective and constructive?

3.6 Team Directory: Vendor Bid Analysis

921. What are you going to deliver or accomplish?

922. Who are the Team Members?

923. When will you produce deliverables?

924. How will the team handle changes?

925. Who is the Sponsor?

926. Who will write the meeting minutes and distribute?

927. Where will the product be used and/or delivered or built when appropriate?

928. Process decisions: how well was task order work performed?

929. Do purchase specifications and configurations match requirements?

930. Who will be the stakeholders on your next Vendor Bid Analysis project?

931. Days from the time the issue is identified?

932. Have you decided when to celebrate the Vendor Bid Analysis projects completion date?

933. Who are your stakeholders (customers, sponsors, end users, team members)?

934. Process decisions: do invoice amounts match accepted work in place?

935. Is construction on schedule?

936. Process decisions: do job conditions warrant additional actions to collect job information and document on-site activity?

937. Who should receive information (all stakeholders)?

938. Decisions: what could be done better to improve the quality of the constructed product?

3.7 Team Operating Agreement: Vendor Bid Analysis

939. What are the safety issues/risks that need to be addressed and/or that the team needs to consider?

940. How does teaming fit in with overall organizational goals and meet organizational needs?

941. Do you solicit member feedback about meetings and what would make them better?

942. Are there differences in access to communication and collaboration technology based on team member location?

943. Do you send out the agenda and meeting materials in advance?

944. Why does your organization want to participate in teaming?

945. Do you determine the meeting length and time of day?

946. Do you use a parking lot for any items that are important and outside of the agenda?

947. To whom do you deliver your services?

948. Are there more than two national cultures represented by your team?

949. Seconds for members to respond?

950. Are team roles clearly defined and accepted?

951. Confidentiality: how will confidential information be handled?

952. Did you recap the meeting purpose, time, and expectations?

953. Do you record meetings for the already stated unable to attend?

954. What went well?

955. What is culture?

956. How will you divide work equitably?

957. Do team members need to frequently communicate as a full group to make timely decisions?

958. Must your members collaborate successfully to complete Vendor Bid Analysis projects?

3.8 Team Performance Assessment: Vendor Bid Analysis

959. To what degree are the relative importance and priority of the goals clear to all team members?

960. If you have received criticism from reviewers that your work suffered from method variance, what was the circumstance?

961. Lack of method variance in self-reported affect and perceptions at work: Reality or artifact?

962. Which situations call for a more extreme type of adaptiveness in which team members actually re-define roles?

963. To what degree do team members agree with the goals, relative importance, and the ways in which achievement will be measured?

964. To what degree are fresh input and perspectives systematically caught and added (for example, through information and analysis, new members, and senior sponsors)?

965. To what degree will the team ensure that all members equitably share the work essential to the success of the team?

966. To what degree are the skill areas critical to team performance present?

967. What makes opportunities more or less obvious?

968. To what degree do team members understand one anothers roles and skills?

969. Individual task proficiency and team process behavior: what is important for team functioning?

970. How hard did you try to make a good selection?

971. To what degree does the team possess adequate membership to achieve its ends?

972. To what degree does the teams approach to its work allow for modification and improvement over time?

973. Do you promptly inform members about major developments that may affect them?

974. When a reviewer complains about method variance, what is the essence of the complaint?

975. To what degree does the teams purpose contain themes that are particularly meaningful and memorable?

976. To what degree are the teams goals and objectives clear, simple, and measurable?

977. To what degree does the teams work approach provide opportunity for members to engage in results-based evaluation?

978. Do friends perform better than acquaintances?

3.9 Team Member Performance Assessment: Vendor Bid Analysis

979. Does the rater (supervisor) have the authority or responsibility to tell an employee that the employees performance is unsatisfactory?

980. What qualities does a successful Team leader possess?

981. What changes do you need to make to align practices with beliefs?

982. To what degree can team members meet frequently enough to accomplish the teams ends?

983. What kinds of performance factors / elements do you use?

984. To what degree is there a sense that only the team can succeed?

985. To what degree do the goals specify concrete team work products?

986. To what extent are systems and applications (e.g., game engine, mobile device platform) utilized?

987. How is your organizations Strategic Management System tied to performance measurement?

988. What are best practices in use for the performance measurement system?

989. In what areas would you like to concentrate your knowledge and resources?

990. Who should attend?

991. What are the standards or expectations for success?

992. What are the basic principles and objectives of performance measurement and assessment?

993. For what period of time is a member rated?

994. How do you currently account for your results in the teams achievement?

995. What evidence supports your decision-making?

996. Is it critical or vital to the job?

997. What is needed for effective data teams?

3.10 Issue Log: Vendor Bid Analysis

998. Do you often overlook a key stakeholder or stakeholder group?

999. Is the issue log kept in a safe place?

1000. How do you manage communications?

1001. What is the impact on the risks?

1002. Who is involved as you identify stakeholders?

1003. Why not more evaluators?

1004. In classifying stakeholders, which approach to do so are you using?

1005. Do you feel more overwhelmed by stakeholders?

1006. How do you reply to this question; you am new here and managing this major program. How do you suggest you build your network?

1007. What are the typical contents?

1008. What is a Stakeholder?

1009. What would have to change?

1010. What is the stakeholders political influence?

1011. In your work, how much time is spent on

stakeholder identification?

1012. Who do you turn to if you have questions?

1013. What effort will a change need?

1014. Are the Vendor Bid Analysis project issues uniquely identified, including to which product they refer?

1015. Why do you manage human resources?

4.0 Monitoring and Controlling Process Group: Vendor Bid Analysis

1016. What departments are involved in its daily operation?

1017. Is there sufficient funding available for this?

1018. How is agile portfolio management done?

1019. How were collaborations developed, and how are they sustained?

1020. How is agile Vendor Bid Analysis project management done?

1021. How many more potential communications channels were introduced by the discovery of the new stakeholders?

1022. Did the Vendor Bid Analysis project team have enough people to execute the Vendor Bid Analysis project plan?

1023. Have operating capacities been created and/or reinforced in partners?

1024. What resources (both financial and non-financial) are available/needed?

1025. Does the solution fit in with organizations technical architectural requirements?

1026. In what way has the program come up with innovative measures for problem-solving?

1027. Is the program making progress in helping to achieve the set results?

1028. User: who wants the information and what are they interested in?

1029. What areas were overlooked on this Vendor Bid Analysis project?

1030. Just how important is your work to the overall success of the Vendor Bid Analysis project?

1031. What input will you be required to provide the Vendor Bid Analysis project team?

1032. Who are the Vendor Bid Analysis project stakeholders?

1033. What do they need to know about the Vendor Bid Analysis project?

4.1 Project Performance Report: Vendor Bid Analysis

1034. What is the degree to which rules govern information exchange between groups?

1035. To what degree does the teams purpose constitute a broader, deeper aspiration than just accomplishing short-term goals?

1036. To what degree does the teams work approach provide opportunity for members to engage in fact-based problem solving?

1037. How will procurement be coordinated with other Vendor Bid Analysis project aspects, such as scheduling and performance reporting?

1038. To what degree will new and supplemental skills be introduced as the need is recognized?

1039. What degree are the relative importance and priority of the goals clear to all team members?

1040. To what degree are the structures of the formal organization consistent with the behaviors in the informal organization?

1041. To what degree will the approach capitalize on and enhance the skills of all team members in a manner that takes into consideration other demands on members of the team?

1042. To what degree can team members frequently and easily communicate with one another?

1043. To what degree do all members feel responsible for all agreed-upon measures?

1044. To what degree are the demands of the task compatible with and converge with the relationships of the informal organization?

1045. What is the PRS?

1046. To what degree can the team measure progress against specific goals?

1047. Next Steps?

1048. To what degree are the tasks requirements reflected in the flow and storage of information?

1049. To what degree is the team cognizant of small wins to be celebrated along the way?

1050. To what degree do team members feel that the purpose of the team is important, if not exciting?

4.2 Variance Analysis: Vendor Bid Analysis

1051. Are all authorized tasks assigned to identified organizational elements?

1052. Are the actual costs used for variance analysis reconcilable with data from the accounting system?

1053. Are authorized changes being incorporated in a timely manner?

1054. Can process improvements lead to unfavorable variances?

1055. Are there changes in the direct base to which overhead costs are allocated?

1056. Are significant decision points, constraints, and interfaces identified as key milestones?

1057. What is the actual cost of work performed?

1058. What is the expected future profitability of each customer?

1059. How does your organization allocate the cost of shared expenses and services?

1060. Who is generally responsible for monitoring and taking action on variances?

1061. What should management do?

1062. What is the total budget for the Vendor Bid Analysis project (including estimates for authorized and unpriced work)?

1063. What can be the cause of an increase in costs?

1064. When, during the last four quarters, did a primary business event occur causing a fluctuation?

1065. Why are standard cost systems used?

1066. Are there externalities from having some customers, even if they are unprofitable in the short run?

1067. Who are responsible for overhead performance control of related costs?

1068. Other relevant issues of Variance Analysis -selling price or gross margin?

4.3 Earned Value Status: Vendor Bid Analysis

1069. When is it going to finish?

1070. Where is evidence-based earned value in your organization reported?

1071. What is the unit of forecast value?

1072. Earned value can be used in almost any Vendor Bid Analysis project situation and in almost any Vendor Bid Analysis project environment. it may be used on large Vendor Bid Analysis projects, medium sized Vendor Bid Analysis projects, tiny Vendor Bid Analysis projects (in cut-down form), complex and simple Vendor Bid Analysis projects and in any market sector. some people, of course, know all about earned value, they have used it for years - but perhaps not as effectively as they could have?

1073. Verification is a process of ensuring that the developed system satisfies the stakeholders agreements and specifications; Are you building the product right? What do you verify?

1074. Where are your problem areas?

1075. Validation is a process of ensuring that the developed system will actually achieve the stakeholders desired outcomes; Are you building the right product? What do you validate?

1076. How does this compare with other Vendor Bid Analysis projects?

1077. Are you hitting your Vendor Bid Analysis projects targets?

1078. If earned value management (EVM) is so good in determining the true status of a Vendor Bid Analysis project and Vendor Bid Analysis project its completion, why is it that hardly any one uses it in information systems related Vendor Bid Analysis projects?

1079. How much is it going to cost by the finish?

4.4 Risk Audit: Vendor Bid Analysis

1080. How do you manage risk?

1081. Level of preparation and skill?

1082. Is the process supported by tools?

1083. Have risks been considered with an insurance broker or provider and suitable insurance cover been arranged?

1084. Are the best people available?

1085. Who is responsible for what?

1086. Does willful intent modify risk-based auditing?

1087. Are some people working on multiple Vendor Bid Analysis projects?

1088. Are requirements fully understood by the team and customers?

1089. What are the risks that could stop you from achieving your KPIs?

1090. Whence the business risk audit?

1091. How will you maximise opportunities?

1092. What impact does experience with one client have on decisions made for other clients during the risk-assessment process?

1093. What are the Internal Controls ?

1094. Do you have financial policies and procedures in place to guide officers of your organization/treasurer/ general members?

1095. Are enough people available?

1096. Has everyone (staff, volunteers and participants) agreed to a code of behaviour or conduct?

1097. Are tool mentors available?

4.5 Contractor Status Report: Vendor Bid Analysis

1098. What was the final actual cost?

1099. If applicable; describe your standard schedule for new software version releases. Are new software version releases included in the standard maintenance plan?

1100. What was the actual budget or estimated cost for your organizations services?

1101. What was the overall budget or estimated cost?

1102. What is the average response time for answering a support call?

1103. What process manages the contracts?

1104. How is risk transferred?

1105. Who can list a Vendor Bid Analysis project as organization experience, your organization or a previous employee of your organization?

1106. What was the budget or estimated cost for your organizations services?

1107. How long have you been using the services?

1108. Describe how often regular updates are made to the proposed solution. Are corresponding regular updates included in the standard maintenance plan?

1109. Are there contractual transfer concerns?

1110. How does the proposed individual meet each requirement?

1111. What are the minimum and optimal bandwidth requirements for the proposed solution?

4.6 Formal Acceptance: Vendor Bid Analysis

1112. Is formal acceptance of the Vendor Bid Analysis project product documented and distributed?

1113. Do you perform formal acceptance or burn-in tests?

1114. What can you do better next time?

1115. What lessons were learned about your Vendor Bid Analysis project management methodology?

1116. How well did the team follow the methodology?

1117. Was the Vendor Bid Analysis project goal achieved?

1118. Do you buy pre-configured systems or build your own configuration?

1119. Was the sponsor/customer satisfied?

1120. Did the Vendor Bid Analysis project achieve its MOV?

1121. How does your team plan to obtain formal acceptance on your Vendor Bid Analysis project?

1122. Was the client satisfied with the Vendor Bid Analysis project results?

1123. Who supplies data?

1124. Does it do what Vendor Bid Analysis project team said it would?

1125. Did the Vendor Bid Analysis project manager and team act in a professional and ethical manner?

1126. What features, practices, and processes proved to be strengths or weaknesses?

1127. Was the Vendor Bid Analysis project managed well?

1128. Does it do what client said it would?

1129. What are the requirements against which to test, Who will execute?

1130. Was the Vendor Bid Analysis project work done on time, within budget, and according to specification?

1131. What function(s) does it fill or meet?

5.0 Closing Process Group: Vendor Bid Analysis

1132. Did the Vendor Bid Analysis project management methodology work?

1133. Are there funding or time constraints?

1134. What areas were overlooked on this Vendor Bid Analysis project?

1135. Specific - is the objective clear in terms of what, how, when, and where the situation will be changed?

1136. Can the lesson learned be replicated?

1137. If a risk event occurs, what will you do?

1138. Based on your Vendor Bid Analysis project communication management plan, what worked well?

1139. Was the schedule met?

1140. What was learned?

1141. What were things that you did very well and want to do the same again on the next Vendor Bid Analysis project?

1142. Is there a clear cause and effect between the activity and the lesson learned?

1143. Is this an updated Vendor Bid Analysis project Proposal Document?

1144. What is the risk of failure to your organization?

1145. What is the Vendor Bid Analysis project name and date of completion?

1146. Is the Vendor Bid Analysis project funded?

5.1 Procurement Audit: Vendor Bid Analysis

1147. Are there established procedures for dealing with and documenting non-performance and return of goods?

1148. Is the performance of the procurement function/unit benchmarked with other procurement functions/units in the different stages of the procurement process?

1149. Are obtained prices/qualities competitive to prices/qualities obtained by other procurement functions/units, comparing obtained or improved value for money?

1150. Were the tender documents comprehensive, transparent and non-discriminating?

1151. Does the strategy include a policy for identifying and training suitable procurement staff?

1152. Do at least two people have custodial responsibilities for negotiable checks (one checking on the other)?

1153. Does the cash disbursement policy prohibit drawing checks to cash or bearer?

1154. Did your organization calculate the contract value accurately?

1155. Were results of the award procedures published?

1156. Has an upper limit of cost been fixed?

1157. Were no charges billed to interested economic operators or the parties to the system?

1158. Does the procurement function/unit have the ability to secure best performance from contractors?

1159. Does the strategy ensure that appropriate controls are in place to ensure propriety and regularity in delivery?

1160. Where applicable, did your organization adequately manage experts employed to assist in the procurement process?

1161. Are travel expenditures monitored to determine that they are in line with other employees and reasonable for the area of travel?

1162. Is there no evidence of collusion between bidders?

1163. Are sub-criteria clearly indicated?

1164. Does the procurement function/unit have the ability to apply public procurement principles and to prepare tender and contract documents?

1165. Are there any complaints of the suppliers and/or end-users?

1166. Do all requests for materials, supplies, and

services require supervisors authorization?

5.2 Contract Close-Out: Vendor Bid Analysis

1167. Have all contract records been included in the Vendor Bid Analysis project archives?

1168. Are the signers the authorized officials?

1169. Have all contracts been completed?

1170. Parties: who is involved?

1171. Has each contract been audited to verify acceptance and delivery?

1172. What happens to the recipient of services?

1173. How does it work?

1174. How/when used ?

1175. Change in knowledge?

1176. Have all acceptance criteria been met prior to final payment to contractors?

1177. Change in circumstances?

1178. What is capture management?

1179. Change in attitude or behavior?

1180. Was the contract complete without requiring

numerous changes and revisions?

1181. Was the contract sufficiently clear so as not to result in numerous disputes and misunderstandings?

1182. How is the contracting office notified of the automatic contract close-out?

1183. Was the contract type appropriate?

1184. Why Outsource?

1185. Parties: Authorized?

1186. Have all contracts been closed?

5.3 Project or Phase Close-Out: Vendor Bid Analysis

1187. Who controlled the resources for the Vendor Bid Analysis project?

1188. What stakeholder group needs, expectations, and interests are being met by the Vendor Bid Analysis project?

1189. What is the information level of detail required for each stakeholder?

1190. How much influence did the stakeholder have over others?

1191. What information did each stakeholder need to contribute to the Vendor Bid Analysis projects success?

1192. Complete yes or no?

1193. Were messages directly related to the release strategy or phases of the Vendor Bid Analysis project?

1194. What are the marketing communication needs for each stakeholder?

1195. Were cost budgets met?

1196. Does the lesson educate others to improve performance?

1197. What are they?

1198. What were the actual outcomes?

1199. What process was planned for managing issues/risks?

1200. Was the user/client satisfied with the end product?

1201. Have business partners been involved extensively, and what data was required for them?

1202. If you were the Vendor Bid Analysis project sponsor, how would you determine which Vendor Bid Analysis project team(s) and/or individuals deserve recognition?

1203. Does the lesson describe a function that would be done differently the next time?

1204. Did the Vendor Bid Analysis project management methodology work?

5.4 Lessons Learned: Vendor Bid Analysis

1205. How much of your time was spent on other than this Vendor Bid Analysis project?

1206. Were the right people available when required?

1207. How effective was Vendor Bid Analysis project Team member training?

1208. How was the quality of products/processes assured?

1209. What could have been improved?

1210. Are there any data that you have overlooked in identifying lessons?

1211. What is the quality and content of communication?

1212. What is the value of the deliverable?

1213. Do you have any real problems?

1214. To what extent was the evolution of risks communicated?

1215. Was there enough support – guidance, clerical support, training?

1216. How useful and complete was the Vendor Bid

Analysis project document repository?

1217. How effective were Vendor Bid Analysis project audits?

1218. How objective was the collection of data?

1219. What specialization does the task require?

1220. What are the external dependencies?

1221. Was the control overhead justified?

1222. Would you spend your own time fixing this issue?

Index

ability 32, 76, 189, 252
abnormal   183
acceptable   45, 91
acceptance   6, 104, 139, 180, 247, 254
accepted   106, 137, 226, 228
accepting   137
access 2, 7-9, 23, 63, 138, 147, 179, 189, 191, 205, 227
accomplish   7, 76, 110, 122, 128, 154, 182, 223, 225, 231
according   36, 38, 152, 191, 248
account   39, 48, 151, 232
accounting   239
accounts   187
accuracy   51, 148, 192
accurate   9, 111, 153, 157, 210
accurately   251
achievable   103
achieve   7, 61, 77, 80, 118-119, 157, 185, 199, 230, 236, 241, 247
achieved   21, 76, 78, 120, 189, 247
achieving   222, 224, 243
acquire   66, 216
acquired   155
across 47, 136
action 47, 49, 90-91, 96, 100, 127, 134, 153, 197, 239
actionable   49, 103
actions 16, 52, 90, 99, 108, 196, 226
actively   194
activities   17-18, 30, 75, 93, 99, 115, 137, 139, 154-155, 157-159, 161, 165, 167, 169, 171-172, 175-176, 189, 198, 223
activity 3-4, 37, 40, 152, 155, 157-163, 167-169, 175, 192, 209, 226, 249
actual 37, 46, 179, 239, 245, 257
actually   39, 63, 86, 181, 229, 241
actuals 173
addition   124
additional   27, 36, 59, 67-68, 71, 140, 153, 177, 196, 226
additions   95
address   21, 83, 172, 181, 217
addressed   127, 135, 163, 193, 198, 227
addressing   32, 109

management 1, 3-5, 8-9, 16, 18, 21, 35, 40, 54, 57, 59, 61, 64, 67, 69, 75, 77-79, 82-83, 85, 103, 113-114, 122, 124, 126, 133-139, 148, 152-153, 165, 169, 171-173, 175-176, 181, 185, 191-193, 195-198, 200, 205-206, 208-211, 214, 216-217, 223, 231, 235, 239, 242, 247, 249, 254, 257

manager   7, 9, 18, 27, 40, 105, 137, 168, 206, 215, 248
managers   2, 125, 135, 168, 201
manages   75, 82, 245
managing   2, 86, 125-126, 130, 195, 224, 233, 257
mandate   132
mandatory   219
manner   20, 76, 152, 237, 239, 248
manpower   191
Mapping   61, 63
margin 154, 240
market 18, 241
marketer   7
marketing   107, 256
material   152, 160, 183
materials   1, 145, 187, 211, 227, 252
matrices   143
Matrix 2-4, 131, 143-144, 187, 201
matter 32, 49, 51
maturing   200
maximise   243
maximizing   111
meaningful   51, 105, 151, 230
measurable   29, 37, 128, 230
measure   2, 9, 19-20, 31, 34, 42-45, 49-50, 52-54, 59, 71, 73, 77-78, 82-83, 91, 96-99, 131, 145, 178, 180, 183-184, 201, 238
measured   43-44, 46, 48, 53, 80, 90, 98, 203, 229
measures   45, 47-48, 51, 53-55, 59, 63-64, 70-71, 75, 91, 97, 99, 203, 217, 236, 238
measuring   99, 151
mechanical   1
mechanics   217
mechanism   147, 195
mechanisms   131, 145
medium   241
meeting   29, 37, 93, 145, 174, 179, 186, 190, 192, 215, 221, 225, 227-228
meetings   29, 33-34, 137, 153, 222, 227-228
megatrends   117

predict 128
predicting   99
prediction   157
predictive   166
predictor   166
predictors   218
pre-filled   8
prepare   208, 252
prepared   176
preparing   172
present   100, 105, 110, 139, 205, 214, 229
presented   24, 218
preserve   29
preserved   70
prevent   53, 167, 191
preventive   203
prevents   17
previous   27, 159, 171, 245
previously   219
priced 151
prices 251
primary   50, 165, 209, 240
principle   212
principles   133, 207, 232, 252
priorities   45-48, 54
priority 48-49, 157, 229, 237
privacy   30, 135
private 133
problem   15, 17-19, 22-27, 29-30, 40, 52, 61, 68, 215, 222,
237, 241
problems   21-24, 82, 84, 88, 90, 109, 141-142, 186, 258
procedure   168
procedures   9, 86, 92, 95, 99-100, 152, 163, 181, 185, 209, 211,
221, 244, 251-252
proceed   187
proceeding   169
process   1-7, 9, 32-35, 37, 39, 41, 51, 57-72, 83, 88, 91-93,
95, 97, 100, 126, 133, 137-138, 141, 143, 145, 147, 163, 167, 175,
180-181, 185-186, 189, 195, 205, 209, 213, 217, 225-226, 230, 235,
239, 241, 243, 245, 249, 251-252, 257
processes   47, 50, 58-62, 64, 66-68, 70, 90, 95, 126, 134, 138,
147, 154, 168, 181, 185, 198, 212, 214, 220, 248, 258
procuring   152

stretch 119
strict   59
strive   119
striving 128
Strongly   10, 15, 26, 42, 57, 73, 89, 101
structure   3, 48, 78, 103, 113, 117, 146, 149, 165, 205, 208
Structured   105
structures   237
stubborn   120
stupid 116
subject8-9, 32
subjective   140
subjects   69
submitted   219
subsequent   153
subset 17
subVendor   199
succeed   50, 114, 231
success   20, 25, 31, 36, 39-40, 42-43, 46, 54, 74, 77, 82, 90,
104-105, 109, 115, 118, 123-124, 128, 133, 196, 199, 206, 215, 221,
229, 232, 236, 256
successful   64, 73, 80, 96, 113, 116, 122, 128, 133, 165, 215,
231
succession   94
successor   153
suffered   229
sufficient   191, 218, 235
suggest   233
suggested   90, 220
suitable   195, 243, 251
supervisor   231
supplier   82, 112, 223
suppliers   41, 62, 122, 252
supplies   248, 252
supply 52, 160
support   7, 20, 66, 81, 94, 96-97, 107, 113, 116, 127, 142,
151, 163, 190, 201, 223, 245, 258
supported   63, 141, 243
supporting   81, 209, 224
supportive   190
supports   232
surface   90
SUSTAIN   2, 74, 101

CPSIA information can be obtained
at www.ICGtesting.com
Printed in the USA
LVHW080000071219
639763LV00016B/454/P